THE GOAL THAT UNITED CANADA

72 AMAZING STORIES
BY CANADIANS FROM COAST TO COAST

BY SEAN MITTON & JIM PRIME

FOREWORD BY DON CHERRY

To Sam,
Enjoy the stories!

The '72 Project ~ What's Your Story?

ISBN # 978-1-300-06109-0

Cover design: Cory Lavalette

Front cover photo: Robert Black

Interior design: Sean Mitton and Cory Lavalette

Photos courtesy of Denis Brodeur, Robert Black, Jim Herder, Hughie Graham, Scott Raithby, Steve Dowling, Marc-Andre Hawkes, Harvey Kirkland and Melissa Pasquinelli.

www.72project.com

Table Of Contents

Acknowledgements

This book is a tribute to members of Team Canada '72 and their families.

Thanks to all the individuals who shared their stories or provided introductions. Your memories have been described with incredible detail and emotion which made the Summit Series feel like it happened last week.

A special thanks to Paul Henderson who has been an ongoing source of inspiration to us throughout the project.

Additional thanks, in no particular order:

Melissa Pasquinelli, Don Cherry, Luba Cherry, Johnny Bower, Philip Belitsky, Rick Howe, Winston Hart, Bill Vigars, Allan Simpson, Peter Scarth, Jim Herder, Society for International Hockey Research, Cory Lavalette, Robert Black, Scott Raithby, David Jull, Paul Henderson, Memorial University, Denis Puska, Canadian Hockey Online, Mark DeMontis, Marilyn Mitton, Pat Cairns, Amy Nagle, Mike Nagle, Paul Patskou, Paul Bruno, Rob MacDougall, Christina Crust, Benoit Clairoux, Bob Young, Dave Watkins, Scott Crawford, Kim Macies, Lauri Gallaway, Michael Browne, Phil Dixon, Judith Coombe, Chad McMullan, Scott Darche, Thad Parker, Dan Zartasian, Paul Mennega, Amon Marstiller, Bob Wage, Al Irwin, Shawn Els, Michael Kydd, Bill Wilder, JP Martel.

Foreword

By Don Cherry

It was the greatest tournament ever played in sports. There's no doubt in my mind about that.

It certainly united our country. We were so behind Team Canada at the time that it didn't matter if you were from the east or west or wherever – as long as we won. That was the main thing and I don't know as we've ever been that way since, I really don't. I know in the Olympics we are a little bit, but nothing like 1972. To me, even the Olympics can't compare to this. Everyone knows exactly were they were when Paul Henderson scored that goal. You can't say that about many things – when Kennedy was shot and that's about it. That's the only other time that I remember as vividly.

I think we were never again as smug as we were before the Summit Series. The way we started out the series, we thought this was going to be a runaway. I think it was a combination of being out of shape, and of scoring two or three quick goals right off the bat. That got us in a bad frame of mind for the whole thing.

And then they come roarin' back, so I did think that after that we started to get into better shape. See, in the old days – and I don't know if it was bad or good – but we used to go for three or four weeks to get in shape. In a way it was a lot better because it took us that long before our first exhibition game whereas now they have the first exhibition game three days after you get there. I say that's why we have so many injuries, you can practice off-line training and everything else. Now we train twelve months a year – which certainly wasn't the case back then. I knew we were in trouble when I first saw the guys because we were definitely not in shape – or ready for them. The Canadians made a joke of the calisthenics and stuff like that. We didn't make fun of their stuff after that!

The line of Ellis, Clarke and Henderson was probably in the best shape of any of the Canadian players. They were "mean tryers" as I call them. They were in the best shape and in the right frame of mind. Sure, they were young but I really think those guys were in pretty good shape anyway, if you know what I mean. They were the types who didn't carouse too much and they are pretty straight-and-narrow guys if you know what I'm talking about. That's one of the reasons. I always liked those "mean tryers." They give it their all, all the time.

The famous photo of Paul after scoring the winning goal captured the joy and happiness on Paul's face. You could just feel it right through the picture. And it's as alive today as when he did it forty years ago. When Paul's at a banquet or even walking down the street people still really want to hear about it. And so they should.

To me, there's no comparison between Paul's goal in '72 and Sid Crosby's at the Vancouver Olympics. Crosby's was a great goal, don't get me wrong. I congratulate Sid the Kid and all that, but I'll tell you one thing: they're going to forget that goal long before they ever forget Paul's. Canadians are never ever going to forget Paul Henderson's goal. And I'll never forget it either.

We had no idea what we up against and to think that we went over there to their country and beat them at their game with everything against us! Everything was going against us. They even said that if the game ended up tied, we lost. We had army guys around us, so to think that we went over there and beat them...

There will never be another series like that. Ever!

❦

Introduction

By Sean Mitton

It's rare in a country's history when people can recall exactly where they were when a long past event occurred. It's rarer still to be able to recall, often in great detail, how they felt and what the event meant to them. Sometimes those recollections are hardwired into our memories during shocking tragedies, like 9/11 or the Kennedy assassination. But if they are powerful enough, positive moments can also take up permanent residence in our hearts and minds, moments like Terry Fox's Marathon of Hope and more recently, Sidney Crosby's Golden Goal that help unite our great country. Some forty years later, the same could be said for the '72 Summit Series.

In the past, stories from the Summit Series have been told either from the point of view of Team Canada players themselves or from the media. The players can certainly offer unique insights, but they are delivered from observers who were at the very eye of the hurricane and therefore often lack perspective. It is the job of the media to add that perspective, but their analytical accounts sometimes fail to reflect the kind of authentic, grassroots passion that enveloped our nation at the time.

This book contains insights from a wide spectrum of Canadians from every province and from a variety of backgrounds. Some were actually involved in the series in one way or another; some attended games in Canada or traveled to Moscow to cheer on their heroes. Some names will be immediately recognizable to you. Most memories are from average Canadians who watched the games on TV or listened to them on the radio. Some younger contributors did not see the series at all but were captivated by it nonetheless. In many ways, those hockey games offer a great opportunity for generations to connect through hockey, a chance to share what life was like back in the early 1970's and reflect on the impact that series has had on the Canada we now live in.

When I explained the concept of this book to friends in the US, they couldn't understand how people were going to be able to recall a sporting event that happened almost forty years ago. In actual fact, collecting memories about the '72 Summit Series has not been a challenge at all. The real challenge has been cutting the stories down to seventy-two. I told the skeptical Americans that Canadians either have really good memories – or this series and this goal *really* meant something to them.

We've tried to select stories that are visceral, show emotion and provide behind-the-scenes insights that you may not have read about elsewhere. It's been interesting to interview people who, back in '72, were not the celebrities we know today. Before Blue Rodeo was a great Canadian band, before Glenn Howard won multiple Brier's, before Terry Fox became a national hero.

For Canadians, hockey has an amazing way of connecting generations and families. I will always remember what Denis Brodeur said to me in regards to rescheduling a call for the next morning. 'My son has a hockey game tonight.' He was referring to his son, Martin Brodeur who was about to play the New York Rangers in the NHL playoffs! If I hadn't known the difference, that comment could have come from any Canadian parent of any hockey player at any level of competition from Pee Wee on up.

When people talk about the series, the first thing that comes to mind is Paul Henderson's goal, a goal that has been replayed time and time again. This book is a tribute to Henderson and all members of Team Canada and their families who made this series a truly memorable one for an entire nation

I can only hope you enjoy reading this collection of stories as much we have enjoyed collecting them.

(Editor's Note: We have tried to present the stories as they were presented to us, with as little editorial intervention as possible. The result is a genuinely representative cross section of Canadian voices.)

🍁

1972 Nostalgia

Population (Estimated)
Canada 22,219,000
Soviet Union 241,000,000

Government
Prime Minister: Pierre Elliot Trudeau
Governor General: Roland Michener
U.S. Watergate Scandal involving President Richard Nixon

Hockey
The Boston Bruins Win the Stanley Cup
Launch of the WHA (World Hockey Association)
Bobby Hull signs first Million Dollar Hockey Contract

Sports (General)
Montreal Expo Bill Stoneman throws no-hitter (October 2nd, 1972)
Hamilton Ti-Cats Win the Grey Cup
Mark Spitz wins Seven Gold Medals at the 1972 Munich Olympics
Eleven Israelis are killed during 1972 Munich Olympics Terrorist Attacks
World Chess Championship, Bobby Fischer (U.S.) defeated Boris Spassky (Soviet Union)

Entertainment
Movie of the Year: The Godfather
Song of the Year: Don McLean's American Pie
Launch of City TV in Toronto (September 28th, 1972)
Canadian Series the Beachcombers first episode (October 1st, 1972)
First Arcade Video Game: Pong

Business
Toronto Stock Exchange Closed at 1,165
Dow Jow Industrial Average Closed above 1,000
Royal Bank of Canada Launches test of 13 ATM's in Toronto, then called 'Bankettes'
Gas was 36 cents per Gallon (estimated)

Notable Births
Canadian Olympian Clara Hughes born on September 27th, 1972
Martin Brodeur born on May 6th, 1972

Team Canada Roster

Coaches: Harry Sinden and John Ferguson.

Goalies: Ken Dryden, Tony Esposito and Eddie Johnston.

Defencemen: Don Awrey, Gary Bergman, Jocelyn Guevremont, Bobby Orr, Brad Park, Serge Savard, Rod Seiling, Pat Stapleton, Bill White, Brian Glennie and Glenn Lapointe.

Right Wingers: Wayne Cashman, Yvan Cournoyer, Ron Ellis, Rodrigue Gibert, Bill Goldsworthy, Mickey Redmond and Dale Tallon.

Centers: Red Berenson, Bobby Clarke, Marcel Dionne, Phil Esposito, Gilbert Perrault, Jean Ratelle and Stan Mikita.

Left Wingers: Vic Hadfield, Paul Henderson, Dennis Hull, Frank Mahovlich, Pete Mahovlich, Richard Martin and Jean-Paul Parise.

USSR National Roster

Coaches: Vsevolod Bobrov and Boris Kulagin.

Goalies: Vladislav Tretiak, Viktor Zinger and Aleksander Sidelnikov.

Defencemen: Aleksander Ragulin, Vladmir Lutchenko, Victor Kuzkin, Aleksander Gusev, Gennadity Tsigankov, Valery Vasiliev, Eugene Poladyev, Yuri Liapkin and Yuri Shatalov.

Right Wingers: Alexander Bodunov, Alexander Maltsev, Alexander Martynyuk, Boris Mikhailov, Vladimir Vikulov and Yevgeny Zimin.

Centers: Vyacheslav Anisin, Vladimir Petrov, Vladimir Shadrin, Vyacheslav Solodukhin, Vyacheslav Starshinov and Alexander Volchkov.

Left Wingers: Yuri Blinov, Valery Kharlamov, Yuri Lebedev, Yevgeny Mishakov and Alexander Yakushev.

'72 Summit Series Scores

Game 1: September 2, 1972
Montreal Forum, Montreal, Quebec, Canada

Team	1	2	3	F
USSR	2	2	3	7
Canada	2	0	1	3
W: Tretiak (1-0-0) **L**: Dryden (0-1-0)				
USSR: Zimin (2), Petrov (1), Kharlamov (2), Mikhailov (1), Yakushev (1) **Canada**: P. Esposito (1), Henderson (1), Clarke (1)				

Game 2: September 4, 1972
Maple Leaf Gardens, Toronto, Ontario, Canada

Team	1	2	3	F
USSR	0	0	1	1
Canada	0	1	3	4
W: T. Esposito (1-0-0) **L:** Tretiak (1-1-0)				
USSR: Yakushev (2) **Canada:** P. Esposito (2), Cournoyer (1), P. Mahovlich (1), F. Mahovlich (1)				

Game 3: September 6, 1972
Winnipeg Arena, Winnipeg, Manitoba, Canada

Team	1	2	3	F
USSR	1	3	0	4
Canada	2	2	0	4
T: Tretiak (1-1-1), T. Esposito (1-0-1)				
USSR: Petrov (2), Kharlamov (3), Lebedev (1), Bodunov (1) **Canada:** Parise (1), Ratelle (1), P. Esposito (3), Henderson (2)				

Game 4: September 8, 1972
Pacific Coliseum, Vancouver, British Columbia, Canada

Team	1	2	3	F
USSR	2	2	1	5
Canada	0	1	2	3
W: Tretiak (2-1-1) **L:** Dryden (0-2-0)				
USSR: Mikhailov (2, 3), Blinov (1), Vikulov (1), Shadrin (1) **Canada:** Perrault (1), Goldsworthy (1), Hull (1)				

Game 5: September 22, 1972
Luzhniki Ice Palace, Moscow, USSR

Team	1	2	3	F
Canada	1	2	1	4
USSR	0	0	5	5
W: Tretiak (3-1-1) **L:** T. Esposito (1-1-1)				
Canada: Parise (2), Clarke (2), Henderson (3, 4) **USSR:** Blinov (2), Anisin (1), Shadrin (2), Gusev (1), Vikulov (2)				

Game 6: September 24, 1972
Luzhniki Ice Palace, Moscow, USSR

Team	1	2	3	F
Canada	0	3	0	3
USSR	0	2	0	2
W: Dryden (1-2-0) **L:** Tretiak (3-2-1)				
Canada: Hull (2), Cournoyer (2), Henderson (5) **USSR:** Liapkin (1), Yakushev (3)				

Game 7: September 26, 1972
Luzhniki Ice Palace, Moscow, USSR

Team	1	2	3	F
Canada	2	0	2	4
USSR	2	0	1	3
W: T. Esposito (2-1-1) **L:** Tretiak (3-3-1)				
Canada: P. Esposito (4, 5), Gilbert (1), Henderson (6) **USSR:** Yakushev (4, 5), Petrov (3)				

Game 8: September 28, 1972
Luzhniki Ice Palace, Moscow, USSR

Team	1	2	3	F
Canada	2	1	3	6
USSR	2	3	0	5
W: Dryden (2-2-0) **L:** Tretiak (3-4-1)				
Canada: P. Esposito (6, 7), Park (1), White (1), Cournoyer (3), Henderson (7) **USSR:** Yakushev (6, 7), Lutchenko (1), Shadrin (3), Vasiliev (1)				

Canada wins series 4-3-1

The Goal That Saved A Marriage

Paul Henderson ~ Toronto, Ontario

As you can imagine, I've gotten a lot of stories over the years. One of the most satisfying came in a letter that was sent to me at Christmas time in 1972. It was from a lady and she wrote that on September 28th her husband came over to where she was living and they were going to sign the final divorce papers.

The third period of the game was just starting and he asked her if he could sit down and watch the game. Now remember, they were definitely going to get divorced and she was going to sign the divorce papers that very day. Well, they start watching the final period and Esposito scored and they cheered. Then, Cournoyer ties it up and they cheer a little more and loosened up a bit. Well, when I scored they went nuts. They were very proud Canadians, and they found themselves hugging each other. He looked into her eyes and, to make a long story short, they had a talk and decided they were not going to divorce that day – and that they really did love one another.

This was at Christmas time and she wrote, 'Paul, thank you for giving me the greatest Christmas present you could have given me, because you saved my marriage. I know that if you would not have scored, my husband and I would have signed the papers, he would have walked out and it would have been all over. Because you scored, we went crazy and we realized we loved each other.'

It doesn't get any better than that!

Waking Up The Underwriters
Vern Aker ~ Toronto, Ontario

During the '72 series, I was fortunate enough right out of Ryerson to land a media position at Manulife in Toronto. At that time, they had installed an internal television studio to produce training videos. I was the newest and youngest of the crew. Being an avid hockey fan, I actually went to a number of the Leaf games at the old Maple Leaf Gardens on Carleton Street. It was the Ballard era so enough said about that! During the '72 series, we decided that if we could get the TV signal into the studio, we could "quietly" let a number of our buddies come down and view it. After much experimentation, remember this was before cable, we finally managed to get the signal in.

So, the last game the studio was packed. Now you have to remember that Manulife at that time was a fairly staid place. So keeping the volume down in the studio was a challenge. Well, all that went right out the window when Paul scored the winning goal. I expect the screams were heard on the 10th floor of our building, amazing since our studio was on the ground floor. Needless to say, we did get a visit from both security and a few higher ups! Thank God they were also hockey fans! Their only complaint was that they weren't invited to the party! Plus I kept my job!

❧

I'll Drink To That!

Jeff Allen ~ Charlotte, NC

At the ripe old age of 20, working in an Olivetti plant in Don Mills, Ontario, they decided to give us the time off to watch the game. My best friend, Gord Dow (God rest his soul) and I drove to my apartment near Young and Eglinton to watch this historic game. We cracked open a couple of Labatts and settled in. What I remember best several Labatt's later was the winning goal, scored by Paul Henderson, and Gord and I jumping up, taking the skin off of our knuckles on the apartment ceiling. We returned to work that afternoon and joined all of the other workers who like us, were floating on cloud 9. My favorite team then and still to this day is the Leafs. We Canadians gather on a regular basis up the road an hour or so in Charlotte, NC, to watch that Canadian tradition Hockey Night in Canada, and share great stories about our homeland. You can take the man out of Canada, but you'll never take Canada out of the man.

❧

Never Give Up
David Altro ~ Montreal, Quebec

My first memory of the '72 Summit Series was having standing-room tickets attending the first game at the Forum in Montreal. I have two distinct recollections of the game. One was that Soviets looked really good in the pre-game skate, and the second thing was that it was really hot in the Forum that day. So hot, that I rolled my pants up.

My dad and I really followed the games closely throughout the series and watched them together. For the final game, I came home from the Concordia University and my dad came home from work. After two periods Canada was losing 5-3 and it wasn't looking good. He said, 'I'm heading back to work.' On his way back, the Team rallied to tie the score and he heard the Henderson goal on the car radio. Unfortunately, it wasn't like today where you could call whenever you liked on the cell phone. He was so overwhelmed with emotion that he cried in his car. I watched the goal at home and felt like I was floating, I was so excited with the outcome of the game! We were two solitudes.

❦

Union Vote Delayed

Jake Bartlett ~ Charlottetown, Prince Edward Island

Back in '72, I was with the Public Service Union in Charlottetown, PEI, and the various provincial government service unions across Canada thought it might be a good idea to combine to form a national union. So the meeting was held in Toronto at the same time as the conclusion of the Summit Series. The last day of that meeting coincided with Game Eight. That very day we were to vote on whether we would have a national union or not.

The debate in the morning revolved around whether we should rush the vote or delay it. Officially, the motion wasn't so that everyone could watch the hockey game that afternoon, but that was really the ultimate purpose of it. So any decision about a national union was put off for a year, really so everyone could watch the game.

That afternoon we went back to the hotel and got together in various rooms to watch the hockey game. I was with a number of others from the Island. We all tried to order room service for food, but no one would answer the phone. Anyone who did actually get the order phoned in, I don't think they ever got it. Not only were all the hotel guests watching the game, but also the hotel employees!

When Henderson scored there was a lot of hoopin' and hollerin' throughout the hotel! Then it was off to celebrate at the bars on Yonge Street. A great day for sure!

The Real Big Red Machine
Irwin Belitsky ~ Montreal, Quebec

I worked for a big investment banking house called Greenshields which became Richardson-Greenshields and then became RBC. I went to Russia in September of 1972 to see the Summit Series. The Chairman of our Board was on the trip, along with our CEO, and when we got home – the very first day we got home – the whole office went into the auditorium and the three of us were at the podium answering questions from everybody in the audience.

They grilled us about the trip, about the games, about the whole experience – because they had been reading about all this East-West confrontation. I was shocked at how big this all was back home. There was no Internet and people didn't know what was happening in Canada. No one used long distance because it was too expensive. Now that seems like it was 100 years ago! You didn't know what was going on in Toronto with the newspaper and TV coverage. We had no TV in our room. There was no satellite. A couple of sports writers in our hotel would hold court in the lobby once in awhile and give us updates – the late Ted Blackman of the Montreal Gazette being one. They told people what was going on because they knew what was happening with the players and the coaches and so on. People didn't know. So it was an adventure – like going to Russia for a holiday and having four hockey games.

They didn't have drug stores in Russia, just the GUM store *(Editor's note: a state run department store of the Soviet era that offered little variety to consumers)*, so in our hotel, the Rossiya Hotel, everyone worked as a team. We brought all our drugs – Advil, Tylenol and so on – to the lobby and put them into a pool so that if anyone was sick – like me with my bad cold and flu – we had access to the whole community stash. Effectively we had a big drug store in the lobby for anybody who needed it, and someone supervised the drugstore. You'd go down and say, 'I need some Tylenol,' and they would give you it from their inventory. That's how a lot of people got through being sick. Everyone contributed. It was a tremendous esprit de corps among all the Canadian people because basically it was us against them. It was the Cold War thing – the Russians against the West.

In 1972, people were still referring to the Soviets as the 'Reds,' red being the colour of the worker's movement. The Red Army was known and feared throughout the world. When I came off the plane into the Moscow airport I had a *Sports Illustrated* magazine and it was about the Oklahoma University football team and the headline said *The Big Red Machine*. Well, I was immediately segregated from all the others. They went through my stuff and put me in a separate room and interrogated me because I had this thing called *The Big Red Machine* which was just an article about college football.

We spent ten days in Moscow and after the series, four days in Leningrad, which is now Petrograd. Every night was another event. One night it was the Bolshoi Ballet and another night it was the opera – and of course four nights of hockey. Our hotel was great and everything was well organized. I think it was the first time that the Russians had hosted 3,000 plus people visiting Moscow for one event, so we had tremendous security all over us. There were people watching us everywhere we went. You really noticed a military and police presence. You also noticed that you were being watched at all times. There was no way you were comfortable walking the streets at night but nobody tried that anyway that I knew of. They went to the games, opera, the ballet, or gymnastics events and were too tired to do much else.

We used bubble gum and Juicy Fruit gum as currency because the Russian people did not have access to that. Whenever we went to a restaurant we noticed that the Russian people were always lining up – long line-ups, always. They were more obedient because of their political environment and they lined up and waited for everything – to buy bread, to eat in a restaurant and so on. But the Canadians just went to the front to identify ourselves and slipped the guy a package of Juicy Fruit or some bubble gum and the next thing you know we were pushed in ahead of everybody. The people who were in line never said a word; they were so obedient because they were trained to their system. You don't question authority. We used a lot of payola of the same kind to get our dinners at our hotel.

Security was tight. For example, every night at the hockey games, there was only one door where you could go in and one door where you could go out. They were lined with military people all the way and you had to walk through this military cordon that they provided. Everyone walked in the same door, no matter where you were sitting in the Luzhniki Arena. All the Canadians sat in one section and in the middle of every row and at the end of every row was a Russian military person. So you had a Russian military person, then about eight Canadians, and then another Russian military person – all the way down the row, just to make sure there were no incidents. The Russian mentality was to have a military or police presence nearby to keep everyone toned down.

During the Alan Eagleson incident, the Canadian players and the fans got up in arms over what was going on – because the Canadians were getting screwed. A goal would go in and the red light wouldn't go on. Things like that. But because of the lack of communications in those days, we were isolated and no one knew what was going on back in Toronto or Montreal or Vancouver or the rest of Canada. We had no access to the newspapers and sports writers. You just went to the game and you cheered for your team.

The Canadian fans cheered and made lots of noise. The Russian fans did nothing. They made no noise, only whistled once in awhile. It was because of their political system. They didn't show any emotions. They were very obedient and followed the rules. They were devoid of personality. It was very obvious, like black and white. I think the arena held 12,000 fans and yet all the noise came from the 3,000 Canadians. Canadian fans were flying the flag and the younger ones were carrying signs from Newfoundland to Cape Breton and Victoria – so many people from across the country – not just Toronto and Montreal, but coast to coast.

In the last game we couldn't really see the winning goal because it was at the other end and we sat behind the net. All three goals in the third period were scored at the other end of the arena. I didn't see the specific play – you just knew that players were at the front of the net and the puck went in.

After the eighth game, the final game when Canada won, we attended a big party in the hotel – all arranged ahead of time – in a convention room/gymnasium and smoked meat had been brought in from Montreal. Rye bread and everything all sliced up and everyone who was there participated in the event.

You may get a different story from sports reporters, but personally I don't think anyone I knew while I was there was so wrapped up in the details – goal scoring and how many goals we had to score to win and how many we had to not let in. The Canadians figured if we won the game, we won and it wasn't life or death. The whole experience was what counted, and you know what it cost? $770, all in! Airfare, transfers, hotel, tickets to all the events. Everything, the whole trip!

When the plane took off from Moscow to fly us home, the whole plane erupted in *Oh Canada*. We were so happy to be leaving Russia. It was such a cold society – grey and black and blue – and big buildings with no style or atmosphere, just big blocks. I myself said I'd never go back to Russia and I never have, nor will I. I've been there and I didn't like it. The Russians themselves were nice. They are a tough people and they have resolve. The people are always nice. It's the governments that cause the problems.

Standing at that podium, I came to the realization that there was more reaction to the series in Canada than there had been in Russia while we were there.

❧

Scoring When It Counts

Robert Black ~ Toronto, Ontario

One of my memories of the '72 Summit Series came before the series even started.

There were three exhibition games that were played at Maple Leaf Gardens with the 35 players on the roster divided into two teams. I had bought a ticket to one of the games and remember sitting in the Greys.

I had brought my camera to the game and decided to move down between periods to get some pictures. Well, I got some great pictures that included Paul Henderson, Phil Esposito, Ken Dryden and Ron Ellis.

During the game, Henderson received a penalty and I remember sitting by the box. I grew up in Kincardine, Ontario, close to where Henderson grew up. I said, 'Paul, score one for Kincardine!' He replied, 'I think I'll save them for the series.' Well...you know the rest.

A Quiet Leader

Johnny Bower ~ Toronto, Ontario

Bower, nicknamed 'The China Wall', won four Stanley Cups with the Toronto Maple Leafs and was inducted into the Hockey Hall of Fame in 1976.

I know exactly where I was. At the time, I was in Vancouver scouting for the Leafs. We checked into the hotel and I knew the game was on and I went upstairs to the hospitality suite and they had a big screen television and I thought *Holy cow, I've gotta watch this!* By the time I got there I had missed most of the game.

When Paul Henderson scored the goal I jumped up and I thought I was going to have a heart attack! I bet there were at least 50 people in that room, travelers and business people, and it just blew their hats off! They just cheered and cheered and cheered and they turned around to me and said, 'Hey Bower, how come you didn't get on that team?' I said, 'I was too young!' They had recognized who I was and I had to do some signing, but that was quite alright. It was a terrific series. Paul's goal affected everyone in Canada.

I knew Paul, of course. I was still with Toronto when Paul came to the Leafs from Detroit. The scout recommended him because he was a pretty darn good goal scorer and that's what Toronto wanted. We were really happy to get him because we needed someone to put the red light on. We finally got one! He was a good hockey player – good skater, shooter, good passer – and the great thing about Paul is that he was so doggone good in the dressing room. You have to have guys like that in the dressing room, older guys especially. The young guys are too quiet sometimes and afraid to say anything. But when you get to a certain age you can say anything you want. Paul was quiet, but he'd make his comments in a soft spoken way.

Ice Dreams

Blue Rodeo (Greg Keelor & Jim Cuddy) ~ Toronto, Ontario

There are some stories that catch you off guard...because they're so remarkable. That can be said of the story from vocalist Greg Keelor of the great Canadian band Blue Rodeo. After describing what the '72 project was all about, I asked him if he was a hockey fan. 'Yeah, I like hockey,' he said casually. After listening to his story, I had goose bumps.

In 1972, I was trying out as a goalie for the Toronto Marlies and we practised at the historic Maple Leaf Gardens. At the end of the tryout, I was the last guy on the ice collecting pucks from around the boards. Team Canada '72 would be the next team to practise. At the end of the rink, the great Bobby Orr steps on the ice. He was injured and didn't play in the Summit Series, but was on the roster. Orr's out there kind of goofing around and taking shots on me. A few minutes later, the Big M, Toronto Maple Leaf Frank Mahovlich, joins in. We played for about 30 minutes. What a memory!

— *Keelor*

Long before Blue Rodeo was on the music scene radar, Jim Cuddy and Greg Keelor both attended North Toronto Collegiate Institute (NTCI). At that time, Jim knew of Greg through football as an acquaintance. He also knew he was a 'hockey guy.' Little did they know that forty years later they would be inducted in to the Canadian Music Hall of Fame.

Growing up, I was a Toronto Maple Leafs fan and I believe Greg liked the Canadiens. The guys I cheered for included Frank Mahovlich, Davey Keon and Carl Brewer.

The day of the eighth and final game of the Summit Series, the school let everyone go early. So we went to my friend Donald Wilkin's house for a party to watch the game. There were probably between 50 and 70 people there, including Greg. We all crowded around the TV and celebrated when Henderson scored!

— Cuddy

❦

The Photo

Denis Brodeur ~ Montreal, Quebec

It is one of the most iconic and instantly recognizable photos in Canadian history: Paul Henderson, arms extended above his head in celebration and exultation written on his handsome face, embraced by teammate Yvon Cournoyer as Vladislav Tretiak lies helplessly in the goal crease and a downcast Soviet player skates past. For the photographer, it was a once-in-a-lifetime opportunity and not one, but two Canadians captured it for future generations. Denis Brodeur was one of them. He also owns a bronze medal as a member of the 1968 Canadian Olympic team for whom he played goal.

I went to Moscow to cover the '72 Summit Series as a freelance photographer. Months before I left, we had our fifth child, Martin (Martin Brodeur has gone on to become one of the great goalies in NHL history). I did a lot of work for the Montreal Canadiens and the *Montreal Gazette*, but for this series, I was working under five different contracts, including one for a magazine, one for John Ferguson, and one for an upcoming book.

One of my concerns going to Moscow was how was I going to develop the negatives in order to get the pictures out? Well, during the beginning of the series, I made friends with a Russian photographer and he helped me get them developed. That was pretty significant as I had over 100 film cartridges. We remained in touch up until the '74 Summit Series, then I never heard from him again. I even tried to connect through Tretiak once.

For the first three games of the series, I shot with a colour and black and white film. For the last game, I didn't want to take any chances, so I just shot in black & white.

I remember the last game we're trailing 5-3 going into the third period and I thought that things weren't looking very good. I was down by the boards between the blue line and the net. One of the photos that I didn't have was of the Russian coach so I vacated my location to get the shot.

Next thing you know Canada scores to make it 5-4, then scores again to make it 5-5.

I had to hustle back to my spot. During the series, I formed goodwill with the Red Army guard by giving him chocolate bars and bubble gum, so I knew that he would look after my spot.

When it came time for the Henderson goal, I had 19 shots left in my camera and used them all for the goal! *(Editor's note: Ironically that's Henderson's number)* I've missed a lot of good pictures in the past by watching and not taking, but I knew that I had this shot! The hockey gods were with me.

Back then you manually had to focus the camera, so I was anxious to see if the photos came out clear. An oddity about the last role of film was that typically you have 36 shots per roll, but on the Henderson goal there were 38 shots.

Standing beside me at the game was Frank Lennon, a photographer for the Toronto Star. He also has a shot of the Henderson goal which is almost identical to mine. Even though we covered for Toronto and Montreal papers, there was never any rivalry. We were friends. *(Editor's note: Lennon passed away in 2006)*

My two favourite shots that I've taken over the years are the Henderson goal and when I was on the ice for Marty's first Stanley Cup. Marty has a framed picture of the Henderson goal in his trophy room, autographed by Henderson. It says something like, 'I'm glad I didn't have to score against you!'

❦

The Luck Of The Draw

Paul Bruno ~ Toronto, Ontario

As a 13-year old in 1972, I remember getting a ticket to Game Two of the Canada-Russia Series. It was a great story. My cousin, eight years my senior, put nine ballots together with self-addressed envelopes to the Maple Leafs to have an opportunity to purchase tickets to the game.

Every ballot holder whose ballot was drawn would get two tickets to the game. We ended up winning with four ballots of the nine that were entered! It was an incredible lucky streak for us. On top of that, the real oddity was that two pairs that were drawn were side by side in the Greys, second row.

We found out about one month before the game. I remember the day because my cousin came over to play street hockey, like many Canadians. He says, 'Guess what?! Four frickin' ballots came through!'

It also happened to be the last game that my father and I would watch live. He usually had a penchant for liking the replays and that sort of thing, but didn't want to miss the spectacle of Game Two in that series.

The added thing about that was after Team Canada got trounced in the first game, we weren't down or anything. We were excited about Game Two. The loss actually added to the excitement because before the series, everyone thought that Team Canada would blow the Russians right out of the water.

The thing that we were acutely aware of as Toronto fans was the fact that Ron Ellis and Paul Henderson would represent the club very well because during the course of the summer – in advance of the series – those two guys and Normie Ulman spent a lot of time getting prepared.

That's one of the reasons why two-thirds of that line, along with Bobby Clarke, turned out to be one of Canada's best lines for much of that series.

Another unusual thing that evening was that the former Prime Minister had a motorcade going to the arena. Lester B. Pearson was a featured guest that night and I believe it was his last public appearance. He passed away shortly after that. We got into the middle of the motorcade down Avenue Road. We were behind the limo with the motorcycles behind us and we sped down that road thanks to the motorcade.

In terms of Game Eight, I missed school because of it. Game Six was also televised at our school and our teacher shut the TV down when Russia took a 5-4 lead. I guess he was upset about the circumstances or the way we reacted and he says, 'That's it for hockey for you guys.' I said to my brother, 'There's no way we're missing Game Eight.' My parents said that's fine and we stayed home from school and watched it in our family room. When that goal went in we just went bananas! It was a great, great memory of ours.

❧

Greatest Tournament Ever Played In Sports

Don Cherry ~ Kingston, Ontario

Cherry is best known for co-hosting "Coaches Corner" on Hockey Night in Canada. Cherry was voted the 7th greatest Canadian on CBC's special, "The Greatest Canadian."

I was coach and general manager of the Rochester Americans and we were playing that night of Game Eight. We had a morning practice and we were out on the ice skating and the trainer came out and said, 'It's tied, you've gotta come in!' We all ran in the dressing room in our uniforms and here we are, these grizzled American Hockey Leaguers, listening to the radio, eh? When Paul scored it was really funny. We were still in our uniforms and we were jumping around as if we'd won the championship! In our Americans uniforms! It was really something.

Actually, I saw the team just before the series and I knew we were in trouble. I went up to Toronto and they were at the Hockey Hall of Fame, and I saw that they were not in shape. You know how the hockey players keep in shape twelve months a year now? These guys, I don't think half of these guys had even skated! I knew we were in a fix and I figured we were going to have problems. The way we started out confirmed it, but the feeling was even worse after Vancouver. Vancouver was the low point of it all, when our own people booed us.

The final result was redemption, I tell ya. It was a really tough series and boy what a relief. I think we were more relieved than happy, if you know what I mean. When you're in hockey all your life – I mean we were *dedicated* to hockey – and all of a sudden the Russians are beating us!? And especially a guy like *me* who was so pro Canadian, you know? And we were getting it from all over. Like from our *own people* we were getting it! 'We're not as good as we think we are' and all that. So it became more than a hockey game – it became their way of life and our way of life. It was the greatest tournament ever played in sports. There's no doubt in my mind.

This is thing that got me. As I said, we weren't in very good shape when we got started, but the more we played the better we got. I think if we'd played another five games we would have been even better. That's what I think happened. The Canadian spirit came through and that's what many of the Russians have said – in fact their head guys have said it: 'We can skate as good as them, we can stick-handle as good as them, we can do everything as good as them – but somehow or other we don't have that Canadian heart that refuses to lose.' And that's comin' from a Russian!

A good word for the Russians is robotic. They had a style coming out of their end, they had a style for everything and they didn't deviate from that style, whereas if you look at how we scored the goals – Esposito bangin' the puck and goin' over to the boards. We innovated. We did it as it came along. It was spontaneous and, you know, Paul – bing-bang and everything like that. So they had their way of coming out of their end – and they've changed now – but back then they were like an army coming out of their end. Well, they *were* the army, whereas we could innovate.

I talked to many of the guys – including one of the trainers, Frosty Forrestall, who was an American believe it or not, but he was the trainer for us. He said you just couldn't believe the tension in the place – with the soldiers and Jean-Paul Parise when they gave him the misconduct. It was a war and I think the guys were awfully happy to get out of there to tell you the truth. It was like a war and I know some people who were over there. They say it was unbelievable, the feeling in the building when we won.

To me it's absolutely ridiculous that Paul is not in the Hockey Hall of Fame. A lot of people think he just scored the one goal. Well he had three winners and seven goals, and he was the outstanding player of the whole thing, and to have the guy in the Hall of Fame who *lost* the last four games and *let in Paul's goal*...he's in the Hall of Fame and Paul's not in the Hall of Fame? Nobody can understand it! Everybody in hockey that I know of, we just can't figure it out. I don't know what they're smokin' when they do that, I really don't. I don't know. I wish I had an answer for it but I know everyone in Canada thinks he should have it. You couldn't get anyone better to represent a Canadian than Paul.

🍁

The Cole Call

Bob Cole ~ Cornerbrook, Newfoundland

We all know the Foster Hewitt call, if not verbatim then darn close. But there was another call of Paul Henderson's Summit Series' winning goal in Game Eight. This one was on radio, and the voice would one day become the voice of Hockey Night in Canada for another generation of Canadians.

'Cournoyer steals it. A pass in front, Henderson...was upended as he tried to shoot it. Here's another shot. HENDERSON RIGHT IN. HE SCORES! HENDERSON! The team pours over the boards. They're mobbing Henderson. They're hugging Henderson. And Kenny Dryden...I've never seen a goaltender do that (inaudible) from one end of the ice to the other, over 200 feet, all the way. And team officials are over the boards. Henderson has got to be the hero of the entire nation now...34 seconds left. They have a 6-5 lead. Can they hang on?' (CBC Radio transcription)

I remember being in a broadcast booth that was not very high up. Compared to the Toronto or Montreal press boxes, it was about 40 per cent as high. The booth that I was announcing from was enclosed with glass. I didn't like that because you couldn't hear the whistles and the sounds of the game. Russian security said they didn't have time to make the changes. Before the game, I loosened the screws, and then Dick Beddoes (*Hamilton Spectator* sports journalist) began to jimmy the glass out. It wasn't long before five or six members of the Red Army were there

– and they weren't going to let that happen. For the final three games, however, the glass was removed.

Every day there was one bus for the media and we all traveled together. Our guide was a Red Army lieutenant. I think her name was Raisa. We always had the feeling that we were being watched.

After the final game everyone was pretty exhausted. It was the end of twenty-seven days, and it was an intense evening. We returned to the lounge at the Intourist Hotel in Red Square. I recall that Foster Hewitt was there with his wife and they had only been recently married at that time. I remember Peter Mahovlich and a few of the other players came by. The win was a tremendous relief.

Meanwhile, we had the feeling that there would be celebrations back home, but we didn't know. There were a lot of telegrams that were sent and they lined the walls by the Team Canada dressing room, so we knew there was a lot of support.

On the way home, we flew from Prague to London and then Montreal. Prime Minister Trudeau was there to greet the players as they landed. Some of the Canadiens got off the plane there – like Cournoyer, Dryden and Mahovlich. (*Editor's note: Some people estimate there were 25,000 people waiting to greet Team Canada at the Dorval airport*)

I was asked to introduce the players as they got out. Afterwards the PM asked when I was heading home to Newfoundland. I said tomorrow morning. Well this was during an election year, and he said to his secretary 'Vic, get Bob's bags, he's coming with us tonight to Newfoundland.' So the Mounties grabbed my bags and I traveled first class with the Prime Minister home. I was the first off the flight and was greeted by many of his Liberal supporters.

It was a really big series to announce, but it was a big series for a lot of media back in '72. With all that was happening politically and hockey-related, I don't think this series will ever be replicated.

❦

A Fateful Goal

Dan Connor ~ Victoria, British Columbia

I have loved hockey since I could tie my own skates, maybe before. I can still remember skating on the ice my Dad had spent hours preparing in our back field in Ottawa.

I was ten years old when my favorite team, the Toronto Maple Leafs, last won the Stanley Cup. I was fifteen years old when my country and my favorite Leaf, Paul Henderson, celebrated the winning goal in the eighth game of the '72 Summit Series. I think it was the most memorable goal and the most memorable game in all of Canadian hockey history. When Paul Henderson scored that goal my love for the game grew tenfold. I would never have guessed that goal and that game would help shape my life years later.

I lived in Victoria B.C. when the '72 Summit Series was unfolding and had faithfully watched all seven games. The night before the final game, as a fifteen year old boy full of oats, myself and a couple of buddies decided to borrow a car without the owner's consent. This was a bad idea. The long arm of the law reached us quickly and the next thing I knew, I was in a youth detention center. Back then they didn't fool around. Not only was I worried about the ramifications of my misdeed, but I was equally worried that I would miss the eighth game of this once-in-a-lifetime hockey experience. I promised myself then and there that if I could see that game I would change my life and somehow get involved with hockey. The hockey gods must have been listening to me as the next morning I was set free. My mother was livid and told me I was staying inside all day. Again my prayers were answered and I got to watch the game. Funny how fate works.

Canada battled the Soviets and I sat glued to that fuzzy screen. Paul Henderson scored the winning goal as I screamed and danced around by myself and I knew then that Canadian hockey history and my personal history had been written.

Fast-forward to the very early 80s when I moved to Edmonton at a time when the Oilers and a young phenom named Wayne Gretzky were on a tear that engulfed the hockey world. The game surrounded me and my brother and I coached my nephew, who as a teen would become a product of the WHL's Swift Current Broncos.

Back to Victoria where I was lucky enough to share my love of the game for 12 years, coaching in the Victoria Minor Hockey League. I loved that page in my life and didn't think things could get much better.

I was hit again by some more fate, this time during my coaching tenure. I was invited to attend a dinner with the NHL Old-timers team that had on their roster my hero, Paul Henderson. I met Paul and he was awesome. He spent his time speaking with me and was a true gentlemen and a truly real person. I have to this day never forgotten that time I spent with him.

I am now 55 years young and have two beautiful daughters who have gifted me with two beautiful grandchildren. I am now waiting for my grandson to become a little older – and if fate and the hockey gods bless me one more time, it may start all over again. My fingers are crossed.

Thank you Paul Henderson and Canadian hockey for helping me shape my life for myself and my family, and hopefully shape the lives of many young hockey players and their families.

I love this game we call our own.

❧

First And Goal

Frank Consentino ~ Hamilton, Ontario

Cosentino was a renowned quarterback who played 10 years in the Canadian Football League (CFL) with Hamilton, Edmonton and Toronto. As a player he was a member of five Grey Cup teams, winning twice with Hamilton.

Cosentino is also known for authoring several books on the history of sport in Canada. Recently he wrote Hockey Gods at the Summit: How the 1972 Canada-Soviet Hockey Summit Became a September to Remember.

I was a teacher and football coach at the University of Western Ontario at the time. Classes stopped and we watched the game in the amphitheater. The challenge was, that day I had to make a presentation at the London High School football championship that was taking place at Western, so I only got to see the first two periods.

There were probably 3,500 students in the stands with many of them listening to the game on transistor radios. After the Henderson goal, the announcer proclaimed on the PA system that Canada won and the place erupted. After that the 3,500 stood and sang the national anthem! We were all proud Canadians!

🍁

How Did A Desk Get Above My Head?
Gary Crawford ~ Chicago, Illinois

When Paul Henderson rescued us from those talented Soviets, I was so happy that somehow I generated enough strength to lift my school desk up over my head! Little did I know (or care) that someone else's books were still inside it.

In addition to them ending up on the floor, so did I.

Most schools (since the final 4 games from Russia were shown live back in Canada) placed television sets in many of their classrooms and in principals' offices. By then, all the lessons focused around this very special Team Canada vs the Soviets Series. If one was in a history class, we discussed communism. If one was in a math class, we discussed how to calculate goals against average. If we were in a language class (English or French), all of a sudden we were taught how to say yes and no in Russian.

Hockey was 24/7.

Because once you got home, all four games were replayed on TV and everyone was once again glued to their set.

Yvan Cournrnoyer, Phil Esposito, Harry Sinden, Vladislav Tretiak and of course "HENDERSON!" not only became house-hold names, but were the centre of the only conversation going on from sea to shining sea.

✤

Memorable Shopping Trip

Darrell Dexter ~ Liverpool, Nova Scotia

The Honourable Darrell Dexter was sworn in as the 27th Premier of the province of Nova Scotia on June 19, 2009.

My mom & dad decided that we were going to go shopping. They loaded all the kids into the car and I was just absolutely mortified that we were in the last ten minutes of the hockey game and they're going to load all the kids in the car and we're going to go *shopping*. We were living in Liverpool, Nova Scotia at that time, so there were was a bit of a drive. I remember mom and dad talking in the front seat and me in the back. I forced them to have the radio on and kept telling them, 'Don't talk!'

The scoring of that goal is not a visual event for me, it is something I heard described. So when people talk about that goal, what comes to my mind is not the pictures, but the sound – and it's kind of neat. It's one of those points in history. It was beyond expectation!

❧

Canada's Wake-Up Call

Gary Doer ~ Winnipeg, Manitoba

Gary Doer is the 23rd Ambassador of Canada to the United States of America. Prior to taking up his current position in Washington, Ambassador Doer served as Premier of Manitoba for ten years.

I was with my buddies watching the final game at one of their houses. I had attended Game Three in Winnipeg. I remember we were down. We thought that, 'Boy, they had a great recovery in some of the losses they had in Canada and this is potentially a bad way to end this great, great hockey series.' But Canada came back and got the tying and the winning goal, and we were all very excited about it because the series certainly didn't start off the way Canada expected!

It was a good wake-up call for Canada. It showed what they had to do to be what we consider the best hockey country in the world. But it was also a good wake-up call for the Soviets at that time in terms of realizing the kind of grit necessary to go to the next level. Of course they won the World Hockey Championships recently, but and I stress the word but, a lot of Canadians were still playing in the NHL playoffs at that time. We'll see in the next Olympics as we still hold the gold medal.

It was a very memorable event for all Canadians!

✦

Celebrating 'The Goal' Twenty Times

Shawn Ells ~ Fredericton, New Brunswick

The Summit Series was a once-in-a-lifetime experience, never to be repeated. Or was it? Shawn Ells, teacher in Fredericton, New Brunswick, wasn't yet born when the iconic series was played. Despite this fact, he got a chance to do something that countless Canadians would love to do. He got to relive the greatest moment in Canada's hockey history when he was cast to play the part of Jean Ratelle in a film about the 1972 Summit Series. The CBC aired the world premier of Canada Russia '72 in mini series format on April 9th and 10th, 2006. The Director was TW Peacocke and head writer was Barrie Dunn.

I had heard a lot about the Summit Series from my father, my brother, and my relatives but I wasn't actually born at the time. And yet I'll never forget it.

When an opportunity came along to be in a movie – and not just any movie but a movie about the Summit Series -I was very interested in auditioning. I'll never forget all the research that went into it. I read a lot of books about it and I was fortunate enough to get the call: 'Hey we'd like you to be Jean Ratelle for Team Canada.' I was thrilled and I can't remember exactly feeling that kind of joy before because I'd never even dreamed of being part of the Summit Series. You can't dream that. It already happened and you don't grow up thinking: Wow, I'd like to be in the Summit Series. It just doesn't make any sense.

It was movie making but it was real at the same time because every morning I was getting up and going to the rink and staying there until late in the evening. We would shoot all day and I'd be wearing my hockey gear. Or we'd be on location somewhere in Fredericton, around town filming at a hotel or the airport. We also filmed in Saint John, but I'll never forget going to the Aiken Centre in Fredericton. One day it would be Maple Leaf Gardens and a week later it would be the Forum in Montreal. Then I'll never forget when it made the transition to become the Luzhniki Arena in Moscow. You felt like you were really there. What a unique experience being around your buddies, all playing hockey, all in character all the time. For those two months I wasn't Shawn Ells, I was Jean Ratelle.

To sum it up, we were a team. We really did feel like Team Canada, and although we weren't playing serious hockey games day in and day out, we were shooting scenes together. We did realize that the Esposito and Henderson characters were busy and they had their role to film, which was not easy. They had a lot of lines and a lot of critical scenes, as you can imagine. We gave them their space when they needed it but by the end of the day we were all joking around and having fun. We were serious, but at the same time we were soaking in every minute of it. It was a lot of fun wearing that jersey day after day.

We definitely picked up on the emotion that had originally existed between the two teams in '72. During scenes we had that hatred too. We could feel it. We didn't talk to the Russian team a whole lot, even off camera. I actually had a couple of buddies playing for the Russians, but when it came to getting the shots – the actual film making – I tried to be in the character of Jean Ratelle. I tried to keep a hate on for the Russians because those were intense games. If you were from Canada, you weren't going to be their friend.

I remember one 'Russian' player that we were quite nice too because he happened to be the film's director, TW Peacocke. He played the part of a Russian defenceman. Not only was he directing but because he was playing the part of a character he was in some scenes. He multi-tasked like no one I had seen before. He did a fantastic job because he was around for the actual series and he remembered it well because he was a big hockey fan.

Prior to the movie, I knew that Paul had scored the big goal. I didn't realize what he'd done leading up to it and how important he was to the team. Dave Miller would actually call Paul on the phone quite often to ask questions.

We did our homework. We knew about the significance of every scene. We watched a lot of film even before we shot a scene. We would watch it closely, the actual game tape. And Booth Savage who ended up playing coach Harry Sinden, he would get us fired up. He was just like a real coach out there standing on the bench because he was into it and he knew his hockey – fabulous actor, who really knew how to motivate and get us going because he was the coach – and he did his part so well.

There was a lot of editing, a lot of scenes shot over and over. To be honest a lot of the guys were actors first and hockey players second. They didn't grow up playing at a high level. There were a lot of other hockey players in the film who were hockey players first, of course, and had never really done acting before so we had a balance there and we found a happy place I guess. We were able to shoot the scenes and sometime it looked good and other times it looked really bad. But that's why there were so many rehearsals and shooting a scene over and over again to get it right.

They used a lot of filming tricks. They brought in about a 100 fans and knew how to shoot the angle and make it look like there were a lot more than there really were, but they used wardrobe of the time – even length of hair and style of hairdos for the spectators . They removed the glass to make it look like Luzhniki Arena where they had high tension netting running around the back of the net. They had the actual advertisers at the time – on the boards from the time in Moscow.

They knew enough not to touch Foster Hewitt's call. They used his voice and I really thought it brought a lot. His voice was the identity of that series – a wonderful call throughout the series.

The day that Henderson scored the big goal was a big day. It was highly anticipated because we knew there were going to be a lot of shots of that scene and I counted about twenty of them. I was actually sitting on the bench with the rest of the team and of course in the last minute and a half of Game Eight, Henderson scored the goal and we celebrated. We all hopped off the bench and joined the celebration and it was all smiles and excitement and jubilation – and then there would be a 'Cut!' And we'd do the whole thing all over again, and again, and again. Before we knew it, we were getting really tired. I really felt for Dave (Miller) who was playing Paul Henderson because he was the one who had to score the goal and he was trying to get it right time after time. He shot it so many times because he knew it was a critical shot and he wanted to get that scene perfect. I thought they did a good job of it.

There was a lot of attention to detail. If you remember when (Pete) Mahovlich was called off the ice by Paul, I wasn't sitting far from him on the bench. I'm taking it all in and thinking wow, this is what really happened. It was really cool to see that. Mahovlich went off, of course, and Henderson came on and the rest is history. The excitement and the exhaustion, just from doing that scene over and over took a lot out of everyone. It was certainly a day I'll never forget. It's like to we had a chance to celebrate the goal twenty times. Usually you count yourself fortunate to see one.

❦

Stopped In Their Tracks

Terry Fewer ~ Grand Falls, Newfoundland And Labrador

In 1972, I was in my last year of high school at St. Mike's. We were in a track and field meet in a small community called Buchans, just west of Grand Falls. When the big goal was scored I was in the middle of a javelin event. It was pretty much pandemonium at the time. The reason I found out about the goal was that they broadcast it over the speakers via radio. I think at the time, there were a bunch of guys running the 100-yard dash. Half way through the race, they quit when the goal got scored. It was pretty neat!

More people at the event were interested in the hockey game rather than the actual track and field event itself. All in all, it was a great day and we got to see the replays that night.

❧

Great Take-Off, But A Bumpy Landing

Ernie Fitzsimmons ~ Gander, Newfoundland And Labrador

During the '72 Summit Series I was working as an air traffic controller in Gander, Newfoundland. I remember watching the game at home that day and I invited a friend of mine, Ivan Manuel, to join me. We were watching the game and we thought, my god it doesn't look good. Then all of the sudden we're tied and Henderson pokes the memorable goal in!

I came off my chair and probably jumped five feet in the air, came close to hitting the ceiling. I came down and hit my chin on Ivan's shoulder and cut my tongue. So, I'm running around with blood running down my face, but I was so happy it didn't really matter at the time. I didn't go to the hospital, but I did put some ice on it and finally got it to stop bleeding. It's still sliced in there a little bit to this day! You can tell it's been bitten.

I think the whole town was watching the game. You could almost hear the roar and see the roofs blowing off the houses!

🍁

Even Heroes Have Heroes

Fred Fox ~ Port Coquitlam, British Columbia

Fred Fox is the older brother of Canadian hero Terry Fox.

Back in 1972, Terry was 14 years old and a big hockey fan. While we didn't play ice hockey, we did enjoy road hockey games. Terry was such a huge fan of both Boston and Toronto. During the series he cheered for Frank and Peter Mahovlich.

At that time, we both attended Mary Hill Junior High School in Port Coquitlam, BC. I remember the whole school was excited and I watched the final game on a TV in the gymnasium. Of course everyone celebrated when Henderson scored the winner.

We returned home from school that day excited and I remember we talked about the game with dad.

Crosby's winning goal in the gold medal game (2010 Vancouver Olympics) brought back fond memories of the Paul Henderson goal.

🍁

23

What I Learned From Tretiak

Peter Friesen ~ Port Albert, Saskatchewan

Pete Friesen is the Head Athletic Therapist and Strength and Conditioning Coach for the Carolina Hurricanes. Friesen has been associated with the Canadian Olympic and international programs for the last 28 seasons, including serving as the head trainer for Team Canada's gold medal-winning team during the 2004 World Championship in the Czech Republic. He again served as head trainer for Canada at the 2011 World Championship in Slovakia, and has now been to 10 IIHF World Championships.

Midway thru the series, Phil Esposito's talk in Vancouver captivated me. He spoke from the heart and said that all the cards were stacked against Team Canada after their tough start. He was one of the guys that got the nation to support Team Canada. It was a showcase event that grabbed the whole country.

It was obvious the Russians were the fitter team, but they were also more creative. From that series, we learned not only the value of fitness, but also creativity in enhancing the potential and skill of Canadian hockey players.

Back then, when we thought about fitness, our focus was on strength and cardio. The Russians showed us different ways to train that incorporated multiple systems in the human body at the same time. I can still picture Tretiak duck-walking and wall-sitting exercises and tennis ball drills.

During the final game, I was in the ninth grade at Prince Albert

Collegiate Institute. I recall the game was around midday and the teacher wheeled the TV into a packed classroom. The black and white reception wasn't great, nothing like today's HD TV's. When Henderson scored, we absolutely jumped up and down. It made everyone so proud to be a Canadian – to appreciate how great the sport of hockey is and its ability to unite the country.

The '72 Series really had a big impact on me. I had always wanted to be a trainer and strength conditioning coach and I recall the first influential book I read was Tretiak's book on off-ice conditioning that came out after the series. In later years, working with Hockey Canada as a trainer at the World Championships, I was thrilled to meet Tretiak in St. Petersburg, Russia.

❧

Waving The Flag For Canada

Lauri Ravenello Gallaway ~ Cape Breton, Nova Scotia

This is the story of how an 11 year old girl from Cape Breton, NS, was responsible for Canada winning the final 1972 Summit game against the Russians.

This will be a short story, as my memories about my life then, even earlier that day, and what happened after, really don't exist.

But on that day, September 28, 1972, I remember the game, and I remember the goal, and how I was personally responsible for the win that day...or so I thought!

I've been asked, 'Why do you remember it?' 'Were your parents hockey fans?' 'Was your brother a hockey player?' No, they weren't. But I do remember that I loved hockey, and I loved my favourite team, the Montreal Canadiens, and I remember the rivalry on the school bus during hockey season about what team was going to win what game. I remember arguing with a girl that her team, the Minnesota North Stars, or as I called them, the Minnesota Door Knobs, were never, ever going to win the Cup.

I guess it was my overall love for the game that had me sitting on the living room floor that day, by myself, glued to the TV, with my little Canada flag in my hand. I watched the whole thing, my stomach in my throat, and in that last period. I started waving my flag. And I didn't stop. I knew that if I did, Canada would lose. And so I waved, and I waved and I waved.

And then it happened. Henderson scored that goal, and the joy and pride of that moment lives on in me like it was yesterday. And, of course,

I knew that it was because of me that we won the game. That was quite an accomplishment for an 11 year old girl from Cape Breton, now don't you think?

❧

First Intermission

Prague, Czechoslovakia. April 18, 1972

This letter of agreement sets forth the terms and conditions that shall govern an exchange of visits between a selected unrestricted Canadian hockey team assembled on behalf of the Canadian Amateur Hockey Association (hereinafter the Canadian federation) and the Soviet National Hockey Team named by the Soviet Ice Hockey Federation (hereinafter the Soviet federation) for the purpose of playing a series of matches in Canada and in the USSR as described below.

The parties hereto mutually covenant and agree as follows:

(a) The Soviet federation agrees that its National Team will play 4 games in Canada during the period September 1 - 8 inclusive, 1972, provided that the schedule includes at least 1 free day for travel or rest between each game.

(b) The Canadian federation agrees that it will send a selected unrestricted Canadian team to play 4 games in the Soviet Union on the following dates - September 22, 24, 26, 28, 1972.

(c) The visiting parties in each case shall consist of a maximum of 30 persons composed of players and officials.

(d) Each federation agrees to be responsible for the transportation of its own team to the other country. Internal transportation shall be the responsibility of the host federation.

(e) The host federation in each case shall be responsible and shall pay for hotel accommodation and meals, while the visiting team is in the host federation's country. The entire visiting parties referred to in point (c) shall be lodged in the same hotel. The respective Embassies of Canada and the Soviet Union shall approve the accommodation to be utilized by the visiting party.

(f) All matches contemplated by this letter of agreement shall be played under I.I.H.F. rules, except that each team may dress 19 players, including 2 goalkeepers for each game.

(g) (i) The officials for all matches contemplated by this agreement shall in the case of matches to be played in Canada, be selected from the U.S.A., and officials for all matches in the Soviet Union shall be selected from other federations in Europe. Such officials to be acceptable to Canada. The officials in any event be acceptable to the parties.
(ii) The host federation shall in each case be responsible for the expenses of the officials for matches played in its federation.

(h) (i) The respective federations hereby mutually agree that for matches played in Canada, the Soviet federation shall receive the sum of $5,000.00 Cdn per match, and that for matches played in the Soviet Union the Canadian federation shall receive an equivalent sum in Soviet currency for each match. The total of such monies in each case shall be deposited as a performance bond with a nominee of each federation in Moscow and in Ottawa, respectively, at the prevailing rate of exchange as at June 1, 1972. Such monies may be released to the respective federations after the completion of each match as set forth in this agreement.

(ii) In the event that either federation shall fail to comply with the terms of the within agreement, then, and in such event, the monies deposited on behalf of the defaulting federation, shall immediately be paid to the other federation.

(i) Each federation agrees to the principle of the exchange of matches as hereinbefore described, and shall use its best efforts to facilitate the implementation of the terms of this agreement.

CANADIAN AMATEUR HOCKEY ASSOCIATION   U.S.S.R. ICE HOCKEY FEDERATION

_____   _____
President

approved
Joe Kearney
(Pres. I.I.H.F.)

A copy of the one page contract for the '72 Summit Series. How many pages would it be today? (Courtesy of Harvey Kirkland)

Paul & Eleanor Henderson during the Henderson Jersey tour. (Courtesy of Eleanor Henderson)

Soviet poster promoting the Summit Series. Notice the Paul Henderson autograph on the puck. (Courtesy of Hugh Graham)

Jim Herder travelled to Moscow for the series and proudly shows off his ticket stubs. (Courtesy of Jim Herder)

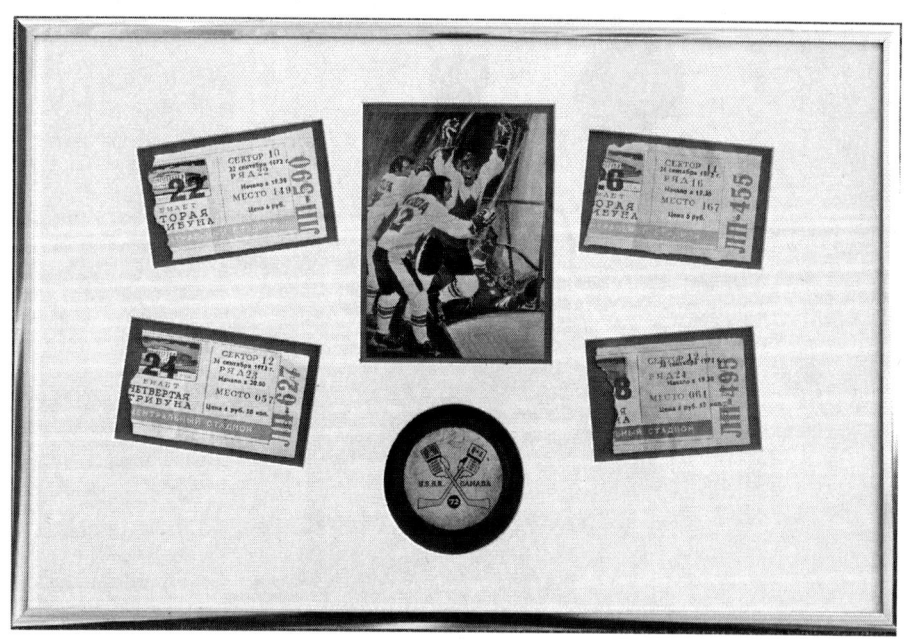

Note the Paul Henderson signed puck. (Courtesy of Jim Herder)

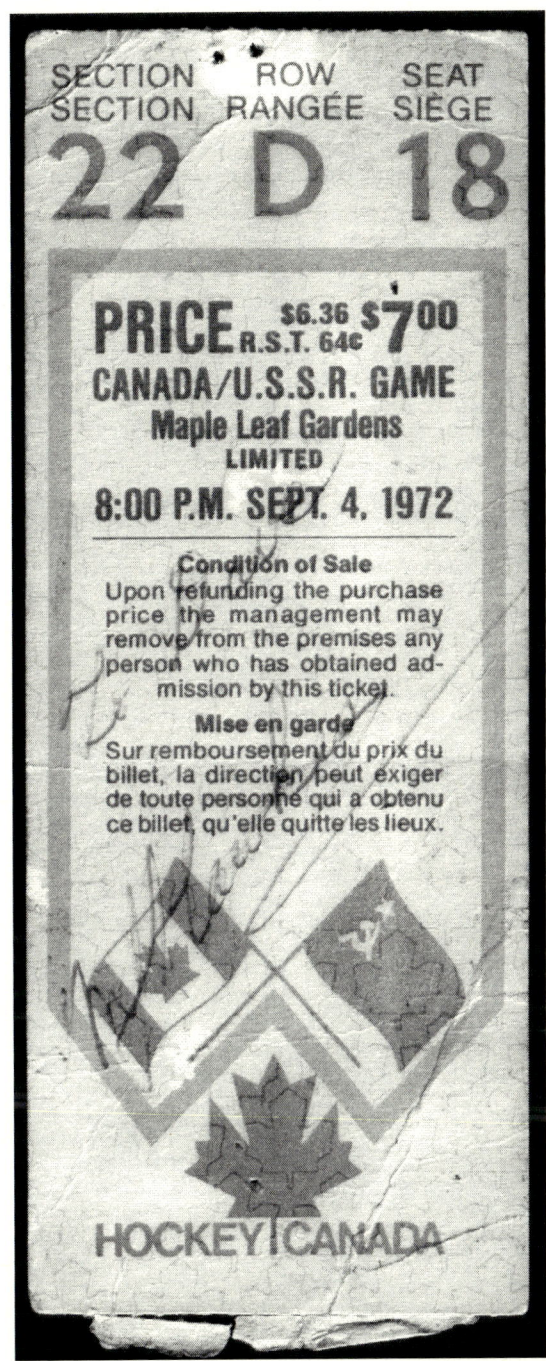

Ticket stub used by Marc-Andre Hawkes' father. (Courtesy of Marc-Andre Hawkes)

Wired For The Game

Richard & Leslie Galpin ~ Coldbrook, Nova Scotia

I had just started working as a lineman for Maritime Tel & Tel (now Bell Aliant). On game day I realized I had no chance of finding a TV 40' in the air...so when I got up in the morning I thought I should take a radio to work...at least then I could hear the game! I then realized the only transistor radio I could find belonged to my girlfriend. This radio had been a gift to her and I was doing my best to take good care of it. When the game started that afternoon, I climbed a pole on Young Street in Truro (NS), over top of the railroad tracks. It was near the end of the game, and I had to keep yelling the highlights to my partner who was on the ground.

Then...the unbelievable happened and Henderson scored! Just as he scored, I reached over to grab the radio that was hanging from a bolt, and in all my excitement it slipped out of my hands, and went crashing down onto the railroad tracks! The end of the game and the end of the radio! When I got down the pole, the radio was in 100 pieces, but it was all worth it, as Canada had won!

You could hear horns blowing everywhere and every car that drove by rolled their windows down to let us know we won! These moments I'll never forget!

Oh yes...my girlfriend must have forgiven me, because we've now been married for 39 years!

— *Richard Galpin*

I actually DO remember where I was during the game.

I was working for the City of Halifax at the time and one of my duties included filing – in what was usually a very quiet room. I arranged my day so I could take a radio to the file room when the game was on, and, as you can imagine, I had so many visitors, I barely got my work done... and yes...the filing room was much noisier that day! When Paul scored the winning goal, the entire department was in the filing room and everyone was cheering!

I later learned that my future husband Richard was up a pole. As for him destroying my radio, it died in a good cause!

— Leslie Galpin

🍁

The Kid With The Radio
David Ghan ~ Raleigh, North Carolina

I was in second grade in 1972. I walked home for lunch every day and was able to catch the games from Russia being broadcast on TV. On the day of the last game, I pleaded with my mom to let me stay home from school after lunch to finish watching. She wouldn't let me and sent me off to school saying 'you know, they'll all be talking about it at school.'

So I walked up to the school grounds all disappointed. I noticed an older kid walking around with a transistor radio against his ear. He was followed by an entourage of about 20 others who were strung along chatting among themselves. The kid with the radio occasionally called back stuff like 'quiet – I can't hear!' He kept on the move, keeping a slight distance from the group so he could hear better. Occasionally, he'd provide a little sparse commentary about what was happening, but I was dissatisfied with the lack of detail.

As the first bell for class rang, the principal of the school spotted the kid with the radio and walked in to school beside him listening along.

Shortly after settling in to class as the teacher began her lesson, the sound of the play by play for the game started, unannounced, on the school intercom. Quiet at first, then louder as the sound was adjusted. The principal had borrowed the kid's radio and was piping it over the intercom! It was so great to hear that! He played it right on through to the end of the game and the whole school in all our different classes sat in our chairs and listened. I think it must have been something like fifteen minutes.

Of course it was great when Canada scored and we all cheered and celebrated. It was a special time we spent together in such a spontaneous way, all fixed in our interest in that game together. It really was something else and I'll never forget that.

❧

Wish You Were Here

Hughie Graham ~ St. Andrews, New Brunswick

I was the only one from my hometown of St. Andrew's NB (pop. 1800) fortunate to go to the four games in Moscow in 1972. Therefore I can say exactly where I was when Paul Henderson scored that historic goal with 34 seconds left. I was in the Luzhniki Ice Palace, a modest arena built in 1956, with about 13,700 seats. On that historic day on September 28th, 1972, 3,000 of those seats were filled with Canadians who made more noise than the 10,000 – plus Russians and their booing whistles. Our steady chant of "Das Das Canada, Nyet, Nyet Soviet" deafened the crowd.

You can imagine our feelings after two periods of that eighth and final game. We were down 5-3 but still enthusiastic – and helped our team claw back to make it 5-5. It's hard to find the words to properly express our jubilation when #19 dented the twine behind Tretiak with 34 seconds to go. When the goal judge was late turning on the huge red light we all screamed at him as Cournoyer and Henderson danced with raised sticks. The 3,000 Canucks in the seats were going nuts, hugging and celebrating and holding our breath as the final seconds were played out. I will never forget where I was on September 28th, 1972.

Dinner before the game was at the Intourist Hotel on Red Square where Team Canada met with us fans as they headed to the arena. I had spotted a huge poster advertising the series at the hotel and had friends raise me up to clip it off the wall. I had it folded in my shirt. As Team Canada marched by I got four signatures on it, two players not playing and two that did. I got Bobby Orr and Stan Mikita, as well as Phil

Esposito and Pat Stapleton as they marched out the door. Later I got Paul Henderson to sign after the fact, to add to the lure of that special piece of heavy paper, treasured by me and my family.

❧

28

Another Great One
Walter Gretzky ~ Brantford, Ontario

Canada's ultimate hockey dad and father to Wayne Gretzky.

No, I don't know where in the devil I was at the time, but we all know about that moment, don't we? Wayne was about ten or eleven, but I can't remember if he watched. That was one of the things that brought Canada together, I truly believe that. It really did, from east to west. No question in my mind. It was absolutely the biggest goal in Canadian hockey history – the biggest ever, ever, ever. There will never be another one like that. Never!

I've met Paul since and he's a good role model. That's what makes it so interesting. It's incredible. I don't know where we'd be today without that goal, honestly.

It changed the game. It changed the fans feelings toward the game of hockey itself. And it's never gone away. It woke all of us up, I really believe that. But the biggest thing was that it brought us together as a real nation.

The game changed, there's no doubt about that. The whole conditioning thing changed, from before the first game was even played. *Everything* changed! Totally! Paul belongs in the Hall of Fame just for that one goal alone, that one incident. That moulded a nation! It brought us to the top and made us realize just what we are and what we have. Prior to that we never thought about what we are and what we had – and have today.

The game of hockey itself changed too, the way we looked upon it and how we approached it. We began to view it in a different sense altogether.

After that goal we were always more prepared. We went prepared for all the games in the series that followed 1972. In '72 we just showed up! We didn't think that anyone could beat us! It woke everybody up, I'll tell you that much. I remember how shocked I was that the Russians could play like that.

If you said to my father, 'Are you Russian, Mr. Gretzky?' He'd say, 'Nyet! Nyet! Bella Ruski! White Russian!' The White Russians were the wealthy landowners who supported the Czar. That's why most of them left – they fled the country. My dad's parents were wealthy landowners. My mother was from Poland, and listen to this: my mother's sister's oldest daughter was living in Toronto since 1991 and I didn't even know it. I met her last year. They were not educated. That's the way the Russians kept the people, as you know, because it made them easier to control. I've since met her and we're now friends.

I didn't really think of my Russian heritage at the time of the Summit Series. I never thought about the connection until just now. The special feeling was that, 'I'm a Canadian and we beat the Russians.' That didn't even come to my mind – that I was a descendant of the Russians. I never ever thought of it. It was just, 'I'm a Canadian and we won! We beat the Russians.' Absolutely no mixed allegiances!

Meeting A Rocket In Moscow
Fred Harrison ~ Georgetown, Ontario

I've been a player in Junior, a minor hockey coach and a lifelong hockey fan. In 1972, I was a real estate agent and during that period I closed a nice deal and decided that I would reward myself and go to Moscow to support Team Canada. I was one of the last people to sign up for the trip.

Like the series, my trip to Moscow had its challenges, but it was all worth it. When I was nearly late for my flight, I found out that it was overbooked. There were fourteen of us who were re-routed to Rome, then Leningrad. We were now the 'group of fourteen,' and we were treated very well for our inconvenience.

Once in Moscow, I recall us landing and going to the bank to exchange currency. It seemed like there was one teller for 1,000 people. There was one Canadian who was overly enthusiastic. At the bank, he started playing a bugle. They didn't like that so much and he was soon taken away by the Red Army. I don't recall seeing him after that.

I attended all four games and had one very interesting experience. One of the people in attendance for the series was the Montreal Canadien great, Rocket Richard. Well, for whatever reason the Rocket didn't have a ticket for one of the games. I gave Rocket one of our tickets and the lady I was with went to the Russian ballet with Rocket's wife. I'm not that interested in celebrities, but it was pretty neat to have sat with Rocket Richard.

The Luzhniki Arena was far from our standards for a hockey arena. We sat at the far end of the rink and I recall that Alan Eagleson was not very popular with the Canadian fans. When Henderson scored, 3,000 Canadians erupted, while the remaining 9-10,000 attendees remained quiet. It was a pretty unique feeling.

It was a long trip home. I remember that a few people on the flight partied, but for the most part we were spent!

Closing The Generation Gap
Marc-Andre Hawkes ~ Edmonton, Alberta

I was born in 1976 and lived in Edmonton, so I wasn't around for the '72 series. I was a huge hockey fan and a big fan of the Oilers in the '80's. I do have a '72 story though. Basically, it concerns my dad. My dad, wonderful individual, great at math and working on cars and so on, but just not a sports guy – unlike his only son who grew up loving hockey and other sports. Long story short, I spent the first 25 years of my life loving sports and yet not talking sports with my dad so much as he wasn't really interested.

After a five month stint studying in Thailand, I flew to visit my aunt in Vancouver. I slept in my cousin's old room. I wake up one morning and I see a billboard on his wall. Lo and behold there is a ticket stub of the 1972 game in Toronto! I was flabbergasted! I didn't know David, my cousin, who was old enough to go at that time, actually went. So I went downstairs to my aunt and said, 'How did I not know about this?' She says, 'Marc-Andre, Dave didn't go the game, your dad went to the game. This is your dad's ticket stub.'

Here I was, about 25 years old, and my dad never told me that he had gone to the game. So, of course I had to call him up and he told me all about it. He said it was a great game, as though it could have been a great local hockey game. Wonderful moment for my dad and me – a complete surprise that was 25 years in the making!

❧

To Russia With Paul

Eleanor Henderson ~ Streetsville, Ontario

As we arrived in Moscow, down in the series, my mindset was that we had something to prove. Not just in hockey, but for our country and systems. We can't go home losers now! I felt we could come back in the series, but you could really feel the pressure and the intensity.

I vividly remember landing in Russia on the tarmac and seeing the Red Army with their guns. I was thinking, 'We have three babies back home. Get me back into the air, I'm not getting off here.' That was the old mentality of the Iron Curtain.

They were not the friendliest bunch and when they took our passports, again I thought, 'What are we doing here?' It was very scary. Many emotions came into play, the fear of the unknown. As far as I know, we were the first professional team to come to Moscow.

Taking the bus to the hotel, I remember the bleakness. It was gray and dull and uninviting. People didn't look happy whatsoever. People were standing in line and we didn't know what they were in line for.

It was stressful and unnerving and you never knew what to expect, because the Russians would throw the unexpected at you. When we had the schedule, there would always be something that came up that would change it. For example, one day we were supposed to have steaks and somehow the steaks disappeared. You never knew what was going to happen next.

Then at the end, the Russians were going to declare themselves the winner if we didn't win based on scoring more goals. Well, where did that come from!? You just never knew what was going to happen.

During that series, Paul was in a different zone. We had been married several years at that time and I had never ever seen this intensity – of him rising to this occasion, to be so absorbed in this whole series.

It all came down to the last period of the series. The intensity! It was *Oh my god, guys you've got to do it! We have to pull this out!* All the wives were a little uptight. You don't want to think doom and gloom, but your palms were a little sweaty and your stomach was in knots. I remember thinking I don't care who scores, just somebody turn that light on.

Looking back at the last minute, it was surreal. I go back and think: How? Why? When he scored I don't think the joy hit right away, it was more relief.

There's a great picture of Paul after the game. He was one of the last guys in the dressing room and he's sitting there in his long johns and he's just spent! It was one of my favourite pictures of him. He gave it his all!

I think back to after the game. We were on the bus going from the arena to the reception, I think the two of us rode in complete silence. It was just such a relief, and to know that he was the one to come through three games in a row. As I said, he was just in a different zone for that whole series.

We really didn't get a sense of the celebrations till we got back to Canada. I came home to signs lined all over our front lawn and all over the house. At that point, you could really get a sense of how much it impacted our country. The impact was far greater than you ever thought it would have been.

Then when the fellas came home, we went to the airport to meet Paul and then went to City Hall for the big reception down there. It just poured rain, what a wild night. Afterwards, when we turned the corner coming down our street, it was just lined with cars and people. It was just such a warm welcome! We couldn't believe the gratitude of the people. The support for the players was amazing.

❦

Worlds Apart

Jim Herder ~ Aurora, Ontario

Where was I when Paul Henderson scored that epic goal in 1972? Seated about twenty rows behind Ken Dryden who was in the Canadian net.

I heard about the Air Canada/Aeroflot trip to Russia late in August, a few days after several of my friends in St. John's, Newfoundland had signed on to go. As a result I was assigned a seat on Aeroflot while they were on Air Canada. At the time I was disappointed not to be with them, but, looking back, I had a completely different experience than they did – and I am glad of it.

We landed at Sheremetyevo International Airport late at night and met head-on with the officialdom of the Communist mentality. Two hours of intimidation, officials searching every one of our bags, checking papers and other manufactured delays led to frustration and created a tension that was unnecessary – but that would stay with us for the full ten days in Moscow.

The bus that took us to Game Five in Moscow was full of highly charged emotion. We started the cheer 'Da Da Canada – Nyet Nyet Soviet' at the top of our lungs and we were ready for anything – or so we thought. As the bus entered the grounds that led to the Luzhniki Sports Palace we looked out the windows in disbelief. Standing shoulder to shoulder were hundreds of soldiers of the Soviet Army. The bus got eerily quiet as it travelled the mile or so in the park leading to the arena. Most of us had probably never seen so many soldiers in one place. It was sobering to say the least. We learned a bit later that it was to protect the

General Secretary of the Central Committee of the Communist Party, Leonid Brezhnev, who was attending the game.

That was not all. In the rink, posted at the end of each row of seats in the section reserved for the Canadian fans, were more soldiers, and they were occupying the seat of the unlucky Canuck who held that particular ticket. As the seats were individually marked on bench type seating, as opposed to individual seats, the Canadian fans simply got that ticket holder to come into the row, then we all pushed against the soldier until he fell off the end of the row. Problem solved.

It seemed the Russian fans seated around and across from us were all dressed in black winter coats. We were wrapped in our flags. Once the action started, the bugles, trumpets and whatever noisemakers we had came out to urge our boys on. The Russian soldiers must have sensed impending revolution, as they waded into the rows to try and confiscate the offending horns. Being inventive, we Canadian fans simply passed the horns up, down and around and frustrated our tormentors.

The fans were coming together as a team. We came from small towns, cities and rural areas from all across our great land. 3,000 of us taking on the Russians. Phil Esposito described it as a war on the ice. And that it was. It was happening right in front of our eyes, and we were the only ones who could help our team.

The Aeroflot travelers were given rooms at Moscow University, as the downtown hotel rooms were all full. Many hockey fans had come from other countries as well. I won't complain about the university food, but it was not great!

One off day, a group of us went exploring around the university campus. We went into the main building and by happenstance ran into a student who spoke perfect English. He offered a guided tour and we gladly accepted. He took us to the top floor to see the sights from the observation deck.

When the elevator door opened, there was another comrade from the military waiting for us. A heated discussion took place, and the student turned to us and said, 'He says there is no observation deck.' We didn't want to get the young man in trouble, so we left. To this day I regret not asking him to join us for a coffee and talking about what it was really like in Russia during the Cold War. I also regret not writing about my experiences for my hometown newspaper, *The Evening Telegram*, where I worked in sales, but it was long before email or faxes, and the thought didn't cross my mind until I was over there, far too late to get press credentials.

My roommate was working with the CBC, and he must have likened himself to James Bond, because every morning when we left the room, he would arrange his belongings in a certain way to see if they had been tampered with during our absence. I kidded him about it at first, but then the proof was in the pudding as the contents of our clothes drawers and closets, were examined every day.

Another time a friend I had made on the plane, Hugh Graham, a postal worker from St. Andrew's, NB had his camera ripped out of his hands on Red Square after he took a picture of the Kremlin. The plainclothes policeman opened the back of the camera, tore out the film and uttered the now familiar "Nyet."

Worse, we were down on the ice, and now faced the daunting task of winning three consecutive games to escape Moscow with a Canadian win. Nobody gave us a chance, the Russian Bears were growing with confidence, and all that stood between them, ultimate victory and world domination – were 20 hockey players and 3,000 frustrated fans, who would ultimately rid themselves of their growing exasperation in the rink.

Henderson had scored the winning goal in games six and seven. Canada 3 wins, Russia 3 wins, 1 tie. Game Eight was for all the marbles. It is the end of the second period: Russia 5 Canada 3. Heads were down in the stands and in desperation someone yelled, 'Next goal wins.' We knew that at 5-4 the Canadians would be energized and all hell could break loose, however if the Russians scored the next goal to make it 6-3, we were toast. So when our players came onto the ice for the third period we all started chanting, 'Next goal wins!' Thirty years later, I ran into Phil Esposito on his way to a reunion the players had at the Royal York Hotel in Toronto.

I asked him, 'Did you hear that chant?'

'You're damn right we did,' he said.

Who scored goal four? Phil.

When I read about the ending of Game Eight some years later, I was amazed to learn that Henderson was not even supposed to be on the ice as the clock wound down, but he spotted Peter Mahovlich running out of gas near the Canadian bench and Paul screamed at him to come off, and jumped on in his place.

Henderson skated into Canadian history, picking up Esposito's rebound and burying the puck behind Vladislav Tretiak with just 34 seconds left. I put my head in my hands and prayed that they would not find a way to attack us once more.

Game over.

We sang *Oh Canada*. I started to leave the arena, only to see a young Russian boy in tears, with his mother trying to console him. I wanted to stop, and try to explain – but I couldn't. We were worlds apart.

Henderson Was Our Favourite

Glenn Howard ~ Midland, Ontario

Glenn Howard is a Canadian curling legend, capturing 4 Briers and 4 World Championships (so far).

I was 10 and my brother Russ was 17 years old during the '72 series. I was a typical Canadian kid who was passionate about hockey.

Before the series started, we felt that Canada would show them whose game it was. But it was surreal how good the Russians were.

The fans were really hard on the players and I remember Espo's speech after one of the games. The team then began to really show its grit and Canadian pride. The Russians may have been in better shape, but our guys dug deep.

For Russ and me, Paul Henderson was our favourite player because we liked guys who skated fast. So his success in the series had us bouncing off walls.

I watched the final game with all my buddies in the gym at Parkview School in Midland, Ontario and went crazy when Henderson scored. I get goose bumps thinking about it.

Looking back on those days, I liked both hockey and curling and eventually chose curling over hockey at age 13 or 14.

♣

Henderson's Exclusive Stick Club: The Gift

Al Irwin ~ Newmarket, Ontario

I was in Peterborough, sitting in my family room in front of the TV like everybody else, when Paul scored the big goal in Game Eight. I figured there was no point in me working. I was employed at Imperial Oil at the time, so I just took the afternoon off and went home and watched the hockey game. I was thrilled with the goal, but then I was so thrilled with Paul in pretty well everything he did. Paul wears his fame so well, you bet he does. He's just one of the nicest guys you'll find anywhere.

Paul's father taught me railway telegraphy because he was a CNR station agent in our hometown – so I knew the family real well. I was not only a real good friend of Paul and his family, but when his father had a stroke and wasn't well, I used to go and give him a hand on the railroad to do the balance sheet at the end of the month. And when Paul's mother died, I was one of the pallbearers. Paul's wife Eleanor and my wife are actually distant cousins. My wife's name was Mary Alton and her name was Eleanor Alton.

The funny thing is – a couple of weeks after Paul returned from Moscow and got back playing with the Leafs, I was down to Toronto for a hockey game and was talking to Paul during the warm-up before the game started and he said, 'Now Al whatever you do don't leave. I want to see you after the game.' After the game I met Paul and Eleanor and we went out for dinner and he said, 'I've got something in the car for you.' He went out and gave me one of his hockey sticks from the Russia series. So I've had that for forty years.

I didn't have it signed when he gave it to me, but his sister and brother just live down the street from us here in Newmarket, and Paul as a kid lived next door to me in Lucknow. I taught Paul in Sunday School. He's just a gem, he really, really is. Paul has really lived his spiritual life, there's no doubt about it. In Sunday School they were young whippersnappers.

One day, I said to Paul's sister, 'You know, the next time Paul drops in, I want him to sign my hockey stick.' This was a few years back. So she phoned here one morning and told my wife, 'Have you got Al's hockey stick? We're going down to Paul's and I'll get him to sign it for you.'

So I came home from work and my wife had forgotten to tell me anything about all this. Well, a knock came to my door and I go to the door and there's Paul's brother standing there with a hockey stick in his hand. I said, 'I can't go out and play hockey tonight, I just got home from work.' He said, 'No, no, this is your hockey stick. We got Paul to sign it for you today.' I thanked him and said that was great. He said, 'You know, Paul took the hockey stick' and he said, 'Where did you get this hockey stick?' I told him I got it from Al Irwin. 'Oh my God,' Paul said, 'That's right! "I often wondered, but I remember I gave it to him because Al was a real good friend of my family." I think he said he had five sticks from the Summit Series and often wondered what happened to that other hockey stick. He was just so excited. "Oh God, am I ever glad that's who it went to!"'

Mark Raithby (see Scott Raithby story) and his family were very, very good friends of ours. Mark was at the Russian series games in Moscow and my brother, who is twenty months older than I am, he and his wife were over as well. When Mark came home he mentioned the hockey stick he got from Paul.

Years later, there was a reunion in my hometown – an old boys and girls reunion and Mark at that time was living in Grand Bend and Paul Henderson was speaking at the Presbyterian Church that day so Mark brought the hockey stick up and got Paul to sign it. And we chatted about it.

Later on, Paul's brother-in-law, Lorne Alton, was going to the hospital in London. His wife had cancer and she was getting treatment and Mark Raithby was there for treatment too. So these guys were sitting there and they got talking and Mark said, 'Where are you from?' and he said, 'Well, I'm from Lucknow.' He said, 'What's your name?' so he told Mark what his name was and they kept chatting and all of a sudden they got talking about Paul Henderson and Mark says, 'You know, I've got a Paul Henderson stick from the Russia series.' He said, 'Paul was skating off the ice and I hollered at him *Can I have your stick?* And he just threw the stick up to me.'

Paul's brother-in-law was at a spring fling here about two or three years ago. I've known him all my life too and he was talking to my wife and Mary said to come and talk to Lorne, he's got something he wants to ask you. So he said, 'Al, what do you know about that hockey stick that Paul had during the Russia hockey series – the one that Mark Raithby has?' I said, 'Oh yeah, as a matter of fact he got it signed by Paul about ten years ago at the last reunion because Paul was speaking at the Presbyterian Church.' He said, 'Yeah that's what he was telling me. You know, he was kind of down when I met him but by god by the time I left him he was right back up.' He was so thrilled that he still had that hockey stick of Paul's. So that's the story on the stick.

I guess when Paul saw the Raithby stick in Halifax, he said something to Mark's son, Scott, to the effect that he wasn't sure it was the one he used to score the winning goal but it was 'one I used there.' I tell you, if you've seen that stick and you look at the one hanging in my basement, you'd recognize it right off the bat because Paul had the ribbing done on it the way he wanted it – the grip on the handle. I can only surmise that it was used in the Russia series. The thing that kind of clarified it was when his brother-in-law brought the stick back to me and Paul had said, 'That's where the fifth stick went.'

I got thinking about the stick again when Paul's sweater was sold (*Editors note: for $1.2 million*). I phoned Paul but he was out that night and I just left a message with Eleanor. I said, 'You know, I've had this hockey stick and it could very well have been a stick that he used.' As a matter of fact I think Paul said that. That's why I called Eleanor. I told her 'I've had this stick for forty years and have gotten a lot of enjoyment out of it but I got thinking – and it never crossed my mind before – but you must have grandchildren that would love to have something like that, so if that's the case be sure to have Paul give me a call.' She said, 'I think the stick's right exactly where Paul wanted it.'

❧

An Aussie Convert
David Jull ~ Scarborough, Ontario

In September of 1972, we were a young married couple with a one year-old infant girl. My wife and I were house and dog-sitting in a home in Scarborough for friends who were traveling. Being in the east end of Toronto, we paid our first visit to the Science Centre. Here, talking into the parabolic sound reflector, we inadvertently made the acquaintance of Michael, a young Australian traveler. We invited Michael to be our guest for a few days.

It was during Michael's stay that the eighth game of the Canada-Russia series occurred. My wife had lived and breathed hockey throughout her life because her dad was Red Burnett, the respected sports writer for the Toronto Star. So this series, which pitted Canadian hockey stars against the cream of Russian hockey, during a period when international politics were all about the Cold War, had real poignancy for us.

By the middle of the series, when Phil Esposito so publicly outlined some of the Russian tactics being used to impede Canada's chances of winning, the Canadian team was clearly cast in the underdog role.

This mix of factors infused the whole series with high emotion and ensured that Michael, the newly minted Australian hockey fan, became inescapably captivated by the drama and intensity of the contest.

When Paul Henderson fired the winning goal past Tretiak, Canada's hockey prowess was confirmed. "Our side" held up its end in the Cold War. Fair play prevailed over dirty tricks. We had the pleasure of playing the vicarious conquering heroes with our new friend.

❦

36

A Brother's Influence
Anne Klisanich (Barilko) ~ Timmins, Ontario

Anne's brother, Bill Barilko, was a 5'11," 180-pound defenceman from Timmons, Ontario who lived a short but dramatic life. Fittingly his career began in Hollywood, California, a PCHL affiliate of the Toronto Maple Leafs. A hard checker, he advanced to the Maple Leafs and played in Toronto for five seasons, four of which resulted in Stanley Cups. In 1951, he scored one of the most famous goals in NHL history in OT of Game Six of the Stanley Cup finals. Later that year he died in a plane crash in northern Quebec. The Tragically Hip later wrote a song honoring Barilko called **Fifty Mission Cap.**

I've been a hockey fan since I was a little girl growing up in Timmins, Ontario. My brother and I used to play floor hockey with a ruler and marbles and we used to listen to Foster Hewitt and the Maple Leafs games on Saturday nights. That's what we did as youngsters.

On February 4th, 1947 we got this phone call. Billy phones home and says, 'Oh Anne, I'm going to play hockey for the Leafs! Ship my clothes to the Westminster Hotel in Toronto.' I knew what the Toronto Maple Leafs were, but I didn't know what the NHL was. They made a big fuss about my brother in Timmins after that. He was in the paper. I said to my friend, 'What's the big deal about Billy playing hockey in the NHL?' He says, 'Anne, you're gonna hear your name on the radio!' I said, 'You mean Foster Hewitt?' and he says, 'Yeah!' I told my mother, 'We're going to hear our name on the radio every Saturday night!'

Of course, we're glued to the radio every Saturday night and I keep getting all these articles from kids who got the newspapers, because we couldn't afford to buy them, so I started making a scrapbook for my brother. What else is there to do in the winter in Timmins? After that I knew what it was all about.

Bill looked after my mother and me and we would come down to Toronto by train to watch some of his games. So that's how I got hooked on hockey. I continued to follow hockey after Bill died and I was always a Leaf fan.

Like Bill's goal, I also remember the excitement of the '72 Summit Series. I'll never forget that time. I was working for the City of Etobicoke and we listened to the games on the radio.

I felt sorry for the Canadian team. They weren't getting the support from the news media and the hockey fans. I remember Phil Esposito and Frank Mahovlich saying, 'What's the matter with you hockey fans? You're not backing us.' So they probably said, 'We'll show ya!' and they did!

It wasn't just our office that celebrated when Paul scored, it was the whole building. I was so happy that Paul did that for our country. I was especially pleased because he was a Toronto Maple Leaf at that time.

It was a wonderful celebration. I agree with so many people out there, that there should be a special place for Paul at the Hockey Hall of Fame. I don't know if it will ever happen, but he doesn't make a very big deal about it. He's very humble, like my brother Bill. He's a wonderful man for people to respect.

❧

Coal War Memory

Marv Koskie ~ Winnipeg, Manitoba

I got to see most of the games, but on the day of Game Eight I was working as a labourer at Kimberly Clarke in Terrace Bay, Ontario. Kimberly Clark was a pulp and paper company but they had a rail line and would bring coal in. They'd open up the bottom of the coal cars and it would go into a kind of bin. They had a chute for getting it out of there. (Being a labourer I wasn't entitled to all the knowledge. It was classified. All I got to know was my shovel) I do know they fired up a whole bunch of this stuff because in those days, forty years ago, coal was the fuel. I'm not sure if it was used on the chipper, to take the bark off, or what. My job was to chuck coal through the bottom of the coal car.

You couldn't see a thing in there because of the coal dust – and I was as black as the coal. All you could see was the whites of my eyes. I had a transistor radio in there and it was really neat when Paul Henderson scored. There I am celebrating inside a coal car and the echoes where just bouncing around everywhere. It was like I was with twenty people I really liked. That's the vivid memory I'll have till I die.

I was surprised at the start of the series but then after the third game, I realized our guys were still in a beer drinking mode. They weren't in shape even though they were pro athletes. The first little while they thought the Russians were just bumpkins and that it would be like beating an AHL team or something. They weren't treating it like a professional sporting event; whereas the Russians, they just kept skating and skating, and so when we left here for Russia I thought, 'Oh boy, we're going to get blown out on the big ice surface.'

I thought that we were very goonish in the series. But I can remember Esposito saying to the country, 'Hey guys, we're trying. We didn't realize they were this good.' By the time they reached Winnipeg they were starting to take it very seriously and were playing themselves into shape.

The last goal by Henderson was maybe one of the ugliest desperation goals ever in hockey. He was swinging wildly. Had the Russian defenceman done his job and hadn't tried to get fancy – if he'd just chucked the puck out – it would have been over. But Esposito gets a bit of a break, can't get a shot, so he flings it toward the net and Henderson was just turning around and gets the goal.

That funny thing was that the Cold War thing didn't matter to me. If anything, I thought it really helped Canada separate itself from the States. It was like we're going to go and play hockey with Russia. The United States and Russia were the ones that were having the real tête-à-tête. Canada basically wasn't in it yet. We hadn't decided that we were that politically motivated, so it didn't really make that much difference to me. I just wanted to watch good hockey.

As far as long term impact is concerned, it put hockey in that next echelon of sports – until the strike, which erased a lot of the good from that series, I think.

♣

38

A Heartwarming Goal

Barb Lane ~ Barrie, Ontario

The Paul Henderson goal was really exciting for us because I was a nurse in an intensive care unit at the Hospital in Barrie, primarily looking after patients that had suffered heart attacks. They all so badly wanted to hear what was happening in the final game that the doctors made a special concession. They decided that they could listen to it because they thought the stress of not knowing what was happening in the game was worse than them actually listening. So it was a good kind of stress when it was all over. When Henderson scored it was pure insanity! In those days when anything was unusual with a person's heart rhythm, beepers went off and everything. So we laughed because every beeper in the unit went off after Henderson scored because everyone's heart rate went up so fast! But it was good, it was positive. I don't recall anyone having bad results from it. Everyone had a positive feeling and we celebrated!

❦

39

Can I Interest You People In A TV?

Gerry Larson ~ Vancouver, British Columbia

Where was I on that memorable Game Eight day?

I was just 22 then and working as a clerk at the CN Telecom office on Granville in Vancouver. The game started in the morning – before lunch as I recall because of the obvious time differences. By Game Eight, Canadian nationalism had kicked in and everyone was talking about "the game." The problem was that it was a work day and our particular company boss was not about to let a hockey game get in the way of work. No radio or TV allowed.

Fortunately, the guy I reported to was a fan and he could see the angst at missing the game all over my face. In those days, one did not call in sick...it wasn't honourable. When I told him I needed to go to the bank during my break he kind of knew it was a stretch. But he let me go anyways. (Thanks Wally!)

And 'go' I did...straight to the 6th floor of The Bay's Granville Street department store where I was sure a TV would be on somewhere in the appliance/furniture area. It was just starting the third period when I got there, and as the game edged on the crowds started to gather and the salespeople started turning on more TV's to accommodate the growing number of fans. I doubt that many TV's were going to be sold at this point.

Before too long the area was packed with fans. When Henderson scored, the place erupted and strangers hugged and shook hands – this was before high-fives – and cried and cheered and cheered some more. I can't recall another time in my life since then that I shared so much emotion with so many strangers as on that day. It truly was a remarkable and very memorable day in my life. It was also clear that I was not the only person skipping out of work!

♦

Oh Canada

Laurine Laxer ~ Key West, Florida

I was home in Winnipeg last year at this time and hockey was EVERYWHERE! When I came back to Key West, my home for the last 24 years, I couldn't beg anyone to watch hockey with me.

No one here, in the southernmost city (tiny island) in the USA, can even imagine what happened that afternoon in 1972, when Paul Henderson scored that goal and Canada, arguably, emerged as the world's Hockey Champion. As a Canadian, it's kind of a birth right, you know and that moment when Henderson scored was absolutely incredible.

I was getting my degree in Poli Sci at the University of Manitoba and I was a Montreal Canadiens fan. Classes were cancelled for the hockey summit, and I watched the entire series in the Arts lounge or the United College Lounge at the University of Manitoba.

It was SOOO passionate. I cannot believe that the Americans that I live with now had no idea of that hockey series, since it was fought and won like a war for us, only on the hockey ice. And what a war it was! Three to three, one tie, and Game Eight.

The ENTIRE staff and student body of the University of Manitoba was in one lounge or another (check through history, how many events cancelled classes like this and you'll find very few), The game was tense. You wanted Dryden to have a shut out but that was a fantasy that died early. It was neck and neck...Cournoyer scored...the damned Russians score...Tretiak was superhuman. (I thought he might have been an astronaut who they bounced out and onto the ice because he was so incredible.)The entire campus! Every person at the University of

Manitoba gathered somewhere in front of a TV Screen for HOCKEY and PAUL HENDERSON SCORED.

We could hear that cheer...starting in Gander, through Glace Bay, up the St. Lawrence, through the great lakes out the prairies and WE JOINED IT.

WHAT A DAY TO BE CANADIAN! What a day for our game!

Trip Of A Lifetime
John Leblanc ~ Garson, Ontario

I was in the school gym watching the game with a bunch of excited kids. My parents were actually there in Moscow, sitting behind the Canadian goalie, half way up the stands. We were living in Garson, Ontario at the time. My father worked underground for INCO. My mother ran a small convenience store called the Jolly Jug and Coke had a promotion for the managers. Every ten cases of Coke she ordered, her name was put into a draw to win a trip to Russia to watch the hockey games. She did win – but they almost didn't go.

Money was tight those days, raising three boys, but they managed to come up with some cash. Their entire group of friends talked them into not missing this trip of a life time, so off they went. My father got a big kick out of hanging with the rich people that went over to Russia to watch the games. He told them that he was into mining: they thought precious minerals, and he meant being a driller at the Garson mine!

Later, I heard a lot of stories about the trip. They stayed in the same hotel that most of the hockey players stayed in. I have a picture of Pete Mahovlich with his arm around my five foot tall mother. One night my parents were woken up by banging on their door, and there was Phil Esposito looking for an ice bucket!

My father recently gave me the team rosters signed by many of the Canadians players, coaches and announcers. I had it framed and will treasure it forever. When asked why he didn't have any of the Russian autographs, he told me they practiced in a different arena and he was scared to travel there.

I asked him what he remembers when the last goal was scored. He said, they all jumped up and screamed, and he actually shook hands with one of the Russian soldiers who was standing nearby. When the Canadians sat as a group, the soldiers were always standing on the steps leading down to their seats – behind them and in front by the glass. Those Canadians must have been a loud, wild group. I was told Canada would cheer and the Russian fans would always whistle. Well, that is a little sampling of their stories. They had a great time and felt very lucky to have been there.

❖

A Tale Of Two Cities

Leonard Leger ~ Memramcook, New Brunswick

I attended the first game of the Summit Series in Montreal. A friend of mine, who wasn't a hockey fan, received two tickets from Air Canada. We flew from Moncton to Fredericton then to Montreal. When we got to Montreal we had a hard time finding a hotel. I remember stopping at the visitor's bureau and my friend pulled out a roll of bills to indicate that he had the money for a hotel. The guy said you better put that away or people will think you're with the Russian mob. Eventually we found one, but it wasn't the best.

I remember the beginning of the game with Prime Minister Trudeau dropping the puck. Canada scored two quick goals and the Montreal Forum was really loud. The Russians came back and they were skating very well. Russia took the lead in the second period and the Forum got very quiet. It looked like our players weren't in great shape. The game finished with a 7-3 defeat. Everyone left talking about the game, and we couldn't believe it! Team Canada was outclassed and I didn't know if they had a chance in the series.

For the eighth game, I was back in Moncton working at the CN warehouse. Our boss decided to hook the radio up to the speakers. He figured if he didn't, everyone would just walk around with radios anyway.

The third period was quite a turnaround, after Canada having being down 5-3. Cournoyer passed the puck to Henderson who was at the right spot at the right time. Everyone hollered when Henderson scored! We carpooled to work so I recall the seven of us talking about the game after leaving work at the end of the day.

The following year I bought an autographed Paul Henderson puck as a memento, which I still have today.

My Personal Team

Tim Lewis ~ Fredericton, New Brunswick

"Henderson scores for Canada!" Those words carry tremendous truth. With the passage of time, it is now clear that Paul Henderson's Game Eight winning goal on the 28th of September, 1972 was more than just a personal achievement; it was more than just the series winning goal for Team Canada; it was something that rallied and inspired a nation on a collective and individual basis. I am one of the individuals who was, and continue to be, inspired by the 1972 Canada – Soviet Union Summit Series. It remains a personal and professional passion of mine to this day.

I was eight years old in September 1972, and from my vantage point as a young hockey fanatic in rural southern New Brunswick, the Summit Series seemed like the most important thing in the world! I was too young to fully appreciate either the political implications of sport in the Cold War, or the extent to which the Summit Series was acting as a spur to Canadian nationalism, but I knew that it was something special. Whether Team Canada won or not *mattered*. They were not just Canada's team; they had become my personal team too!

Like everyone else, I experienced a roller-coaster of emotions over the course of the first seven games of the Series, so I could not wait for the eighth and deciding game. Sadly, the elementary school I attended was not one of those that brought televisions into the classrooms allowing students to watch the game. Happily, I arrived home after school in time for the start of the third period. Things seemed rather bleak, "we" were down 5 to 3, but Team Canada had already bounced back from a two-game deficit in the series, so hope remained. We know the rest of the story. "Henderson scored for Canada!"

As a long-suffering Toronto Maple Leafs fan – insert joke here – the conclusion of the Summit Series remains the most joyous moment I have ever experienced in a sporting context. But it has become so much more than that. It serves as an ongoing reminder of how great obstacles can be overcome when all seems lost. As a person of faith, I have been inspired by Paul Henderson's spiritual journey that was, in many ways, triggered by his experience in the '72 Series. Even my career in now linked to '72.

I teach Canadian history at Vancouver Island University (VIU) in Nanaimo, BC. As a lifelong hockey fan and history buff, I dreamed of one day developing a course that would examine Canadians' relationship with the game of hockey. A few years ago, that dream came true. I now offer two, third-year history courses at VIU centered on the theme of "Hockey and the Canadian Identity." The '72 Series is a major component of the second of those courses, sub-titled, "Canada's Game in the Cold War and Beyond."

Sometimes I have to pinch myself that my work now revolves, in part, around an event that has brought such joy to me over the years. I truly am blessed. It is also deeply satisfying to have an opportunity to share with new generations of Canadians what the '72 experience meant to this nation. And, I am happy to report, students are almost as passionate in learning about the series as I am about teaching it. For me, the '72 Series lives on in multiple ways. "Henderson scores for Canada!"

❧

Carleton University Celebration
Kevin MacLeod ~ North Sydney, Nova Scotia

Kevin S. MacLeod is the Usher of the Black Rod for the Canadian Senate, the Canadian Secretary to the Queen of Canada and the author of the historical fiction novel, A Stone on Their Cairn/Clach air An Càrn.

I was an undergraduate student at Carleton University attending a political science class at the Saint Patrick's Campus. It was a really important class for some reason or another and most of us knew that we could not "skip it" even though we were more than cognizant of the importance of the game that was being broadcast on CBC. We also knew that there was a TV showing the game in the student lounge on another floor.

We were about half way through the class when an ungodly, yet very sweet sounding, roar or cheer went up. Many of us raced out of the classroom to the lounge and managed to join in the revelry – at least for a few scant minutes. And then it was back to the classroom. We celebrated in greater style late in the day, but any recollections of the precise nature of the subject matter being discussed in the class that day had escaped me. However, the memories of first hearing that glorious cheer and racing to the lounge remain with me still as, I hope, they always will. It was truly a great moment for Canada.

♣

Hard To Be A Journalist That Day

Peter Mansbridge ~ Winnipeg, Manitoba

In 1971, Mansbridge moved to Winnipeg as a reporter for CBC Radio, and in 1972, joined CBC Television. He became chief correspondent and anchor of The National in 1988.

I was a young reporter in Winnipeg at that time and had just been in the business a couple of years. I remember that day pretty clearly because I was assigned to go out and visit a few schools and watch them watching the game. And so I did that and I had to come back to the studio, and those were the days of film where you had to get the film to the lab to get it processed before you could edit the story. For that reason, we'd left before the game was over and I can remember being in the newsroom for the third period and the sort of sag in the newsroom because they were losing at the beginning of the third period. And then how they kind of caught up, and then how Henderson who was probably the most unlikely of candidates because you usually think in these big games, the hero of them will always be some superstar. Henderson was known but he was not a superstar.

Then, as you know, he had the winning goal in the last three games and that remarkable last minute when he scored. I mean it was just like... people were screaming and yelling and it was crazy. And this kind of feeling that everybody in the country had and the kind of pride...

It was hard to be a journalist that day because people were so caught up in it. It was such a unique championship in a sense because we'd never played the Russians on that level as pros and we were used to always losing at the amateur rounds to them. But we thought we were going to thump them, and then suddenly it was unbelievably tight and we were coming back and it was just an amazing story.

It kind of united the country. One of those things that hockey does for Canada is that you suddenly find out, around certain things like the Stanley Cup often, but certainly at that time, where you could pretty well point to anyone across the country and you knew they were all watching the same thing. That doesn't happen very often in our country, as big as we are and as diverse as we are. But on that day, they were, and whether it was in a little school in Winnipeg or somewhere else in the country you knew it was that kind of feeling. That's my story.

❧

The Golfer, The Wager And Bobby Orr

Brian McFarlane ~ New Liskeard, Ontario

Brian McFarlane is well known for being a commentator on Hockey Night in Canada *for twenty five years. He has written more than fifty books on hockey.*

I was hired by Hockey Canada to be a public relations liaison between Hockey Canada and the Allan Eagleson Group. That sounded like a good idea at the time, but I found out very quickly that there was a lot of friction between the two parties. I felt like I was really caught in the middle, maybe not earning my keep. The Eagleson Group kind of took over and took control and made decisions. While I wasn't left out in the cold, I felt a little uncomfortable. While I managed to emcee a couple of banquets, I felt my role was not very well-defined, you might say, and I didn't like to take money I wasn't earning. After four games, I decided to pack it in and go home. That seemed to be fine with everybody, so that's just what I did.

I was with *Hockey Night in Canada* at that time. We were disappointed – and I think I speak for all the guys – that we didn't get the rights to the series. I think *Hockey Night in Canada's* bid on the series was quite low. Eagleson felt, along with Harold Ballard and others, that it wasn't enough, so they formed a group with CTV and Johnny Esaw and I think they garnered a lot more for the rights than we were willing to bid. As announcers, we felt like we lost a trip to Moscow for one thing, and we felt it would be a series we'd really like to be a part of, but only Foster

Hewitt and Howie Meeker from our group were hired to be a part of the telecast team.

I always felt the series would be a lot closer than a lot of other people did. In fact, I made a bet with one of my colleagues. He was willing to bet me $20 on *every game* that Team Canada would win by ten goals. I thought it was ludicrous. In any series – even playing against Juniors – I felt ten goals was an awfully wide margin. So I accepted the bet, but I never got paid off on it.

Like everyone else, I watched in fascination as the series unrolled. Team Canada made the great comeback in Moscow that culminated with Henderson's goal.

Before the first game in Montreal, I sat in the stands with Bobby Orr for the morning skate. I recall Bobby watching the Russians coming out in their tattered uniforms. They looked substandard and their skates looked a little second rate too. We all commented that they looked like some kind of Senior D team, really. I remember Bobby turning to me and saying, 'Look at the way they line up for their shots on the goalie. They move in from 10-12 feet out, our goalies would be screaming at us if we did that!'

Most of the people in the stands felt that it was going to be a really one-sided confrontation. That night I had a rink-side seat at the Forum. I sat beside one of the female golfers from Quebec who was a tournament player back then, and she had brought a friend from the LPGA along. Well for this friend, it was her very first hockey game. It was a revelation to sit beside someone who was seeing their very first game, a game that happened to be a terrific comeback by the Russians against Team Canada in the opener of the Summit Series. What a stunning surprise to the whole nation. I think she was blissfully unaware of all the ramifications and what was happening in people's minds around her. How many people, with knowledge of the game, would have loved to be sitting in her seat?

At the beginning of Game Eight, I was at home and someone started the vacuum cleaner. Well, I decided to head to the local bar, which was about a mile away, and watched the game with a bunch of strangers inside the Bayview Village Shopping Mall in Willowdale.

It dramatically changed hockey. I think we started out with an arrogant bunch of thirty-five players, far too many, we finally realized that. They thought they were going to have a party atmosphere for a month or so – first in Canada then in Moscow – then be lauded for their great achievement in walloping the hell out of these guys, who were World Champions. We realized later they were superb hockey players and every bit as good as we were in many ways. We were fortunate to emerge as victors in this series and we were arrogant to think we could send guys over there who weren't in shape. We quickly realized in the first game we were in for a battle.

A few years ago, I might have thought it was interesting that Russians were now top NHL draft picks. Now we expect the Russians to be in the top ten juniors in the draft – every year.

🍁

A National Treasure
Liam Maguire ~ Manotick, Ontario

On September 28th, 1972 I was in grade eight at St. Leonard's Elementary School in Manotick, Ontario. Manotick is a small village nestled on the Rideau River about fifteen miles south of Ottawa. It's grown considerably since then. St. Leonard's was an elementary school that went up to grade eight at that time, so I was starting my last year of grade school as we called it. As I recall it was a beautiful early fall day. In those days, we actually had four seasons, unlike the melting pot of weather we experience circa 2012.

It was a Thursday afternoon, Game Eight was scheduled to start around noon our time, and one of the students in our class, Billy O'Brien, had asked his father to drop off a TV for our class to watch the game.

Two days earlier for Game Seven, the senior grades, which included our class, were allowed to watch in the gym and we saw Canada win on the most amazing winning goal maybe ever scored in the sport of hockey from an aesthetic point of view, with a mere 2:06 to go in the game! Paul Henderson had continued his hot hand and recorded his fourth goal in the three games played in Russia, this one coming as he went around or deked out the entire Russian team before falling and roofing the shot over the Soviet goalie, Vladislav Tretiak. He was on fire! The gym was filled with pure elation as Canada hung on and now Game Eight meant something. We all said as we left the gym we'd never see a more dramatic goal scored ever again.

Thanks to Billy O'Brien's father we were able to watch Game Eight in our class as opposed to the gym. Our teacher, Mr. Pat Jennings, gave specific instructions. If you wanted to watch the game, the TV would be set up at the back of the class room. If you chose to go outside for lunch or for recess that was your decision. You would then have to do school work. Those watching the game in its entirety were exempt from any school studies.

The game was tied 2-2 after one and Canada was trailing 5-3 after two, leaving a lot of us dejected. The refereeing was so one-sided that it seemed an impossible hole to climb out of, but all of us played hockey and we all knew a quick goal in the third would or could turn things around. Phil Esposito's goal was great but Yvan Cournoyer's to tie it was just incredible. He was my favourite all-time player – still is – so I was beside myself when he scored, even though it seemed as if it might not count, as no goal light went on. This created the wildest scene you'll ever witness in the history of hockey, with Alan Eagleson having to be rescued from the Soviet military, who had guns, by Canadian hockey players, who had hockey sticks. Through the broken, black and white satellite transmission, we all were transfixed by what was happening thousands of miles away.

As I think back now, when Henderson scored, it's just impossible to describe the feeling. The very first thing I saw, next to jumping in the arms of my buddies was my teachers – Mr. Pat Jennings, Mr. Lyle Bergeron, our principal, Mr. Bob Slack, in the hallway jumping in each other's arms. I can picture this so clearly. I was 13 years old, it was 1972 and you had total respect for your teachers to the point where they were almost god-like. I remember for a brief moment feeling a little scared at the unbridled enthusiasm they were showing. I remember that so well. Then it was back to the set for 34 more seconds which seemed like 34 years. I just could not believe we won, absolutely could not believe it and could not believe Paul scored again. It was then, and remains to this day, the most incredible moment I've ever seen in sports.

Paul Henderson became an immediate hero of mine during that series. All the players did, but with his goal-scoring exploits – especially in Russia – I just knew one day I'd have to meet him. I finally got that opportunity on Monday night, December 4th, 1995. I was a guest on a national CBC show, The Pamela Wallin Show with Paul, noted journalist Roy Macgregor, and the late Carl Brewer.

I came on the show halfway through, just past the bottom of the hour, so it was 9:30 pm EST. As I came on the set, I finally had a chance to shake his hand and thank him for what he did for our country at that time 23 years previous. I remember looking at the clock the exact time I shook his hand, 9:31 pm. I note this because it's the exact time my father passed away, 9:31 pm, Monday night, December 4th, 1995. He had been battling terminal cancer and I was not even going to go down to do the show, but my mother insisted. I only found out the next day from my brothers what time dad had died and ever since then it's my belief that Paul and I are linked spiritually. He was and still is an inspiration for me, especially now as he fights this dreaded disease, leukemia. My father was my hero, he will forever remain my true hero, but on September 28, 1972 at 2:30 pm EST, the 19:26 mark of the third period in Game Eight of the greatest, most unbelievable series ever played in the history of sport – Paul Henderson also became a hero. Not only to me but to ten million plus Canadians. He is a national treasure, an icon and more importantly a gentleman in the truest sense of the word. I have run a national campaign to hopefully see him with both the Order of Canada and induction into the Hockey Hall of Fame.

❧

Accountants Gone Wild

Mike McLew ~ Toronto, Ontario

The morning of the day of the final game, I remember distinctly. I worked with a firm of about 4,000 accountants called Ernst & Young. It was very difficult to get a colossus like Ernst & Young to move any direction, least of all, if it had to do with sport. So on this fateful morning, I was so excited. Incidentally, I'm not an accountant but perhaps this is the reason the story evolved like it did. I became so excited about the prospect that we were going to play Russia, in Moscow, the eighth game of this incredible series and we were tied 3-3. There was no one seemingly, paying very much attention, certainly in terms of the partnership. We had about six floors at that time in the Royal Trust Tower in downtown Toronto and so I said to one of the operational guys I knew, 'Go out and rent six or seven TV's so that we can put one of those in each boardroom and then we can invite all the staff to watch the game.' So off they went to rent these TV's and we mounted them all, one per boardroom per floor.

The game started I think shortly after lunch time. I have to tell you there were moments in the afternoon when faint voices were heard from the senior partners saying, 'Where the hell is the staff?' But it didn't matter, because everybody was entranced with the incredible happenings of this game and it was a most wonderful experience. You could hear the cheers going up from floor to floor. And that from a firm of 4,000 accountants, I can tell you was a totally unique experience!

❧

Second Intermission

Denis Brodeur poses with his photos of the Henderson goal.
(Courtesy of Denis Brodeur)

Toronto photographer Frank Lennon with Denis Brodeur. Great location!
(Courtesy of Denis Brodeur)

Photographers Frank Lennon and Denis Brodeur. (Courtesy of Denis Brodeur)

Referees left to right: Steve Dowling; Gordon Lee; Frank Larsen; Len Gagnon during training at Maple Leaf Gardens in Toronto. (Courtesy of Steve Dowling)

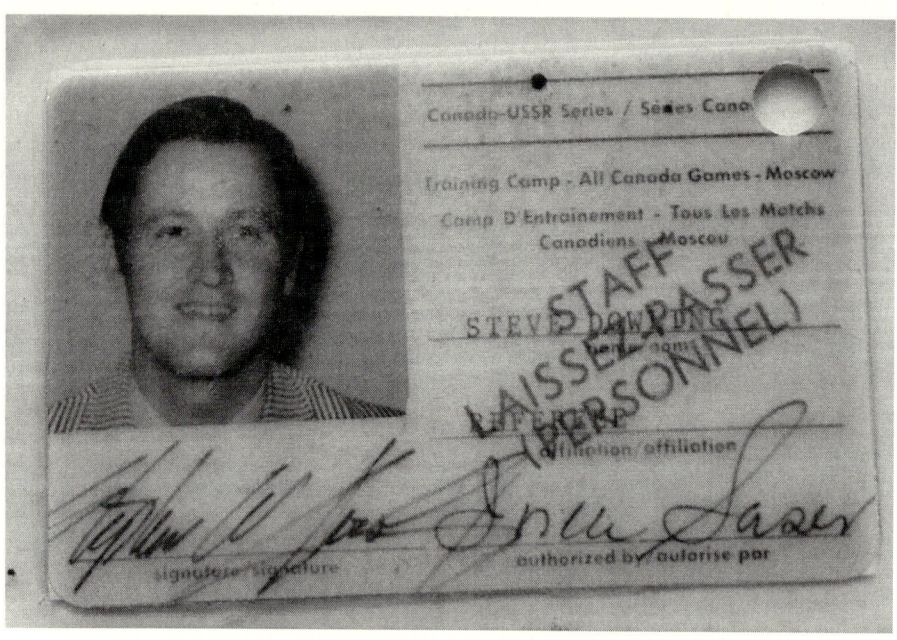

Dowling's training camp security pass. (Courtesy of Steve Dowling)

*Paul Henderson & Scott Raithby share a laugh during the Henderson Jersey tour.
(Courtesy of Scott Raithby)*

*The Raithby's celebrate with Paul Henderson at a reception following Game Eight in
Moscow. (Courtesy of Scott Raithby)*

Luzhniki Arena present day. (Courtesy of Melissa Pasquinelli)

Puck that Steve Dowling pocketed from Game Two in Toronto. Team Canada won 4-1. (Courtesy of Steve Dowling)

49

Omega Man Hears Muffled Roar
Paul Meade ~ Wolfville, Nova Scotia

Unfortunately, I had a chemistry lab the afternoon of the game and when I walked out to head back to my residence at Acadia University, it was like I was the Omega Man, the last person on the planet. The campus was silent and barren, not a soul in sight. The chirping of the birds was all I could hear on my lonely ten minute walk back to my room. As I headed up the path to the high-rise resident building at the south end of campus, I looked up at the column of windows facing me, and I could see people in the TV lounges glued to the game.

Suddenly, I was shaken from my silence to hear the loudest roar I have ever heard from inside a building. It was an odd, muffled roar that broke the solitude of my lonely trek. Then came the jumping up and down that I could see through the windows of each floor. To my surprise, I could hear muffled roars coming from all the other residences surrounding me. The roars could only mean one thing: Team Canada scored the winning goal. While I was possibly the only human being standing outside when Paul Henderson scored that goal, I have the unforgettable memory of hearing the most deafening, muffled roar I will ever experience.

And at least I got to see the replay!

❦

Canada Played With Heart And Brains

Howie Meeker ~ Kitchener, Ontario

Meeker played for the Toronto Maple Leafs for six years, winning four Stanley Cups, but he may be best known for his colour commentating on Hockey Night in Canada during the '70's and '80's. He was inducted into the Hockey Hall of Fame as a broadcaster in 1998.

Before the 1972 series, the Canadians had no idea how good the Russians were, and they wouldn't listen. I had told them because I had seen them play before I came home from the war. I bet 90% of them played soccer. They were over for a tournament at Wembley Stadium and the Canadian army had a hockey team there as well. I was part of the hockey team and we were practicing and the Russians were watching. Eventually we got them on the ice – got them sticks and skates and equipment and, oh, they could fly. Actually they were better – *all of them* – with the puck than any one of us – and we had some pretty good hockey players.

In '72 in Moscow, we were in this gondola affair to broadcast the games. It was great to be with Foster Hewitt. He was really super, but I think the best chances I had were between periods. There was no replay or anything else to show, just a still picture on the screen. I had to provide an explanation of what was going on.

Prior to the big goal, I was up in the broadcast booth with Foster (Hewitt), which was halfway up the arena, and I had a post-game show that I had to do down in the corner, sitting in amongst the fans. It was just madness leading up to Henderson's goal. The score was tied 5-5. I was in the middle of the arena on my way down to the corner. When I got into the corner, Esposito had the puck – he had outfought two Russians for it – and he threw it out in front. Henderson shot and Tretiak went down and made the save and the rebound came back to Henderson and he put it in.

Suddenly, I was halfway up the screen! I can remember being half way up because at that time they didn't have glass, they had a plastic kind of screen. I was about halfway up that – about a foot above the goddamn rails or boards, hollerin' and screamin' like everybody else. Halfway up the screen! And in the corner where all the Canadians were too! It was at the other end of the ice and gosh we all went nuts!

In my mind, until the eighth game, I was kind of hoping the Russians would win, so that it might wake Canada up – that we had to teach skills at the lower levels. But Canada deserved to win, you're goddamn right they did. Esposito won it for us. He wouldn't quit. None of them would quit. And some of the fellows that I didn't think would ever make the Hall of Fame – everybody in that eighth game played up to Hall of Fame and better standards. That Pat Stapleton, short little defenceman, holy Jesus, he was just super! And we were lucky as hell because Dryden had been very, very average through the whole series. And we're down two goals going into the third period and I'd say the first ten minutes the Russians had three or four excellent scoring chances and he stoned them all! Had they beat him there, three goal difference and the game would have been over. His performance there matched everyone else's performance on the ice. The whole Team Canada played extremely well but Esposito was the heart and soul of that team.

We knocked their best player out of the series on purpose with a slash to the ankle – the little right winger (Valeri) Kharlamov. Bobby Clarke of Philadelphia, on orders, put him out and no one in the rink saw it. That's the amazing thing. I'd never heard *anybody* say he saw the slash, so it had to be way out of the play and down in the corner, back-checking or something like that, with the puck way ahead of them or way behind them. It wasn't in the area of the puck at all. Nobody saw it.

The reaction of the Russians when Paul scored was not bad (chuckles). They didn't think it was possible they were going to lose it. In fact they didn't think it was possible to lose after they left Canada. They thought this was going to be a shoe-in. They had won the first game in Russia and only lost the second by a close score, but Canada was coming and by the eighth game had really reached their physical and mental capacity to play the game. They were top-rated at that point.

Everyone on the team played like hell, and played with their brains and played with their bodies and played with their heart.

When we got back home it was just crazy. We had no idea – none of us in the press corps – and in TV had any idea of how worked up Canada was! (CBC producer) Gordon Craig was the fellow in charge of getting the games back to Canada – and fighting with the Russians about what he could do. They were trying to dictate what we could send back and what we couldn't send back and Gordon Craig said, 'Up your ass! We're sending this back and that's it.' He was in contact with Canada all the time and he came back and said, 'Hey fellas, the whole country back home – everything's stopped and everybody is watching and it's gone crazy.' It made you very, very proud to be a Canadian and to be part of hockey. I was in Newfie at the time and people were crazy when I got back. It's a hockey island. That's about all they have in the wintertime – hockey and snow and rain and drizzle and fog.

It was a wonderful thing to be part of. I got to know Foster really well when I was with the Toronto Maple Leafs. He thought the Canadian effort in the Summit Series was outstanding. He told me that he'd never seen a Canadian team play the game better.

Personally, I don't think there's any comparison between the Summit Series and Canada's Olympic win, although that was big time too. It was to a different audience. There are hundreds of thousands of young people who had never seen that quality of hockey and never had a chance before to get enthused about the game – and enthused about Canada!

❦

Radio Days

Marilyn Mitton ~ Georgetown, Ontario

When I was a child living in rural New Brunswick we had no electricity. I remember sitting around the radio on a Saturday night to hear the hockey broadcasts in the days of six teams and well-known players. One's imagination was alive and vivid!

Now it's September 28th, 1972 and I'm the mother of two young children on that momentous day. Even then it was not the TV, but the radio that was turned on to get the buildup and hype to that final game of the Canada-Russia Series. I had kept abreast of the previous games through newspaper, radio and TV news, but on that day, there was no question...I was going to listen to the game on the radio.

I would describe myself at that moment, not as a hockey fanatic but a cheerleader for our hockey team and for Canada, full of hope and expectation for a thrilling outcome. Totally into the game, picturing the dynamics through the announcer, I paced the floor, listened for the children to wake from their afternoon naps, tried to putter in the kitchen with supper preparation...and in short, was a nervous wreck. I remember at one point near the end of the game where I thought I was going to have to shut it off, I was in such a tizzy with a crazy racing pulse and heart beat!

Then, the moment!!! At the peak of my emotions, I jumped up and down and immediately started weeping...for joy! I couldn't stop crying! I thought Paul Henderson was the most famous human being in that instant! Then, I recall thinking that I had to talk with or tell someone, so I ran out the back door to my next door neighbour, scarcely able to tell her what had happened. I'm sure she thought I was crazy! I don't think I had ever experienced such a euphoric sensation in my whole life to that moment.

It was not to be repeated again until the Canada Winter Olympics final Canada-USA game and the other famous goal, by Sidney Crosby.

Oh yes, I remember it well!

❧

Heart Of A Lion

Rick Moffat ~ Montreal, Quebec

Moffat is a Montreal radio announcer, providing play-by-play commentary on CJAD for the Montreal Alouettes.

Like many Canadians, I felt a mix of shock, outrage, and pride at Team Canada's performance in the opening games of the series. But those emotions would be stirred again for Game Eight.

Our high school principal deemed that all who wanted to watch the fateful game could gather in the gym to watch live from Moscow as hockey history was written in *Canadian Red and White* against the *Soviet Red Menace* (It was actually all pretty *Black and White* in our school). The principal qualified his popular decree with word that – of course – this decision was at the teachers' discretion.

Only problem was that: my science teacher for the fateful class would not let us out. He had immigrated to Canada from East Africa, and while he had us in awe by revealing a scar on his arm he claimed was from the swipe of a lion paw, we were stunned at his failure to grasp this moment of national pride.

For every goal, our science class could gauge the wild exuberance or audible distress echoing from the gym. A pride of lions couldn't have roared any louder when Henderson scored.

Recently, I met Paul Henderson and Vladislav Tretiak at the Bell Centre before a Canadiens game. 'The hockey world won that day,' suggested Tretiak. 'No', I thought. 'Canada did.'

❧

A Touch Of Hockey Heaven

Mike Nagle ~ Mississauga, Ontario

Imagine this was you: standing alongside Paul Henderson, getting your picture taken with him on the ice in Luzhniki Arena, at the end of the very rink where he scored "the goal." That is where I was in November 1999. How did I get there you say? Well, let's just say that stars aligned one day...

It was in the spring of 1999, I was sitting in Tim Horton's, large regular in hand, and talking hockey with a good buddy from our men's recreational church hockey team. In walks our goalie's dad, Glen, and he sits down at the table next to us. We exchange some small talk and then he proceeds to read through his emails (hard copies). After about 10 minutes he hands an email over for me to read. It was from Ilya Bantseev, a Christian Missionary over in Siberia. In the email, he describes how he had met Paul Henderson a year prior and had mentioned to Paul that it would be great if he could bring a men's recreational hockey team over to Siberia to help build bridges between the church and the community. Hockey is what Siberians lived for nine months of the year and he thought it would be a great way to bring hope to the community.

After retiring from hockey, Paul Henderson went into full time Christian ministry and he and Glen worked together with Ilya and several other missionaries overseas. At that time, I was working at a large church as a youth pastor and was heavily involved in our men's church hockey teams, both competitively and recreationally. When Glen saw this email he thought I would be the perfect person to work with Paul to bring a men's hockey team over to Siberia for some friendly recreational games. My jaw literally dropped! At the time, I had never met Paul although, of course, I knew who he was and that he lived close by. I was only two when he scored, but I lived that series over and over again vicariously through my dad who was a huge hockey fan. Me...traveling to Siberia with Canada's hockey icon...I was honoured, intimidated and speechless...this can't be happening!

The next meeting was in a boardroom with Paul, Glen and me and everything took off from that point! Fast forward to November of 1999... there are 20 or so hockey players – with varying hockey backgrounds from recreational to ex-pro – our coach, trainer & translator joining Paul Henderson at Pearson Airport in Toronto on our way to Siberia, with a brief stop in Moscow to go visit Luzhniki Arena.

During the planning stages and while we were traveling to Russia with Paul, I had often wondered how the Russians viewed him. We revere him across Canada as the one who scored "the goal" and united our country. Did they see him in a negative light? Did they even know who he was? Well, when the plane landed at our destination city, that was answered pretty quickly. There were police escorts for our team bus everywhere we went, ceremonies with gifts and autograph seekers. Paul kicked up quite a stir!

I will never forget eating dinner one night with the team in the hotel restaurant. There was a dull roar with all of the conversations going on and then in bursts this Russian with a big smile and open arms yelling 'Paul Henderson!' as if he was ready to give him a hug! Trailing him were a couple of his friends. He then went into a rant in Russian that no one could understand until our translator interpreted it for us. He said that he had heard that the Canadian hockey star from the '72 series was in town and that he just had to meet him. It turned into an impromptu autograph and photography session and 10 minutes later the man and his entourage were gone. Has to be one of the funniest, strangest things that happened on that trip.

It was certainly a dream come true for every guy on that trip. Although only two players had previously ever played professionally, the rest of us felt that we touched a bit of hockey heaven!

🍁

54

Meeting Adjourned

Bob Olivero ~ St. John's, Newfoundland And Labrador

Olivero is a former MUN Fellow and James Channing was Clerk of the Executive Council of Newfoundland, from 1955 to 1978

In 1972, I had returned home following three years in Africa to teach at Memorial University School of Business. Before that could happen, I had been dragooned by Dave Mercer to work that summer on COGAP, the committee reorganizing the public service following the PC ouster of the Smallwood administration. Half the committee was MUN colleagues and all were MUN graduates except for Jim Channing, the Chair and Head of the Newfoundland Public Service, who had articled as a lawyer. Jim was a very keen sportsman and hockey fan.

The committee and consultants had worked and met steadily throughout the summer and into September. (And eventually worked up 'till Christmas.) That schedule conflicted with the Canada-Soviet hockey series and especially the famous "Henderson Goal," Game Eight at the end of September. Our meetings at the Confederation Building that month were regularly punctuated by roars and cheers of the staff watching and listening to the games throughout the building. Poor Jim Channing would squirm and grimace each time he knew he had missed seeing a key play or goal. But he was the model of a British bureaucrat: disciplined, honest and duty-bound to stay the course. Finally, I believe during a ruckus and fight just before the Henderson goal, he could stand it no longer and abruptly adjourned our meeting and rushed out to watch the game in a flurry of papers and documents.

❧

The Stars Were In Alignment

Percy Paris ~ Halifax, Nova Scotia

Percy A. Paris is a Canadian politician and member of the Nova Scotia House of Assembly in Halifax, Nova Scotia. Paris currently serves as the Nova Scotia Minister of Economic and Rural Development and Tourism.

I could almost tell you where I was for every game during that '72 series. I had just finished my first year at St. Mary's University in Halifax, where I was playing hockey for the SMU Huskies. I used to spend my summers working for the City of Halifax as a summer student and I was living in Ogilvie Towers, a low income apartment building in the South End.

My job with the city involved a lot of outside work where I had a city vehicle and was doing traffic counts and that sort of thing. I always made sure that when the hockey games were on I was home in front of my 19-inch black and white TV. And you may recall some of those games were on early in the afternoon. I watched every game.

I watched the games by myself and my wife was actually bringing meals to me so I didn't have to leave the TV set. I was planted there, like millions of other people, I'm sure. This demonstrates for me the power of the game of hockey. I am an eighth generation person of African descent. I'm a Canadian. Hockey is that sport here in Canada that doesn't look at you in terms of where you are born, what religion you are, what the pigmentation of your skin is. You grow up in Canada loving the game of hockey and for many of us, it is a way of life. There's this immediate bond, this immediate respect when you play hockey against someone.

When Paul Henderson scored his goal, I, along with thousands of other people in the city of Halifax, screamed – you couldn't hear me scream because everyone else was screaming at the same time! I still remember that whole series so fondly and for those of us who were old enough, what a Canadian experience that was! And Paul Henderson, of all people, and I say this in a very complimentary way, of all people to score that goal. It was befitting that it would be him. Here you've got this Christian soul who through so much hard work – and I don't want to take anything away from the other players – but it just seemed so fitting that Paul Henderson would score this goal. I remember also some people back in '72 questioning some of the players who were on that team. Paul Henderson was probably one of those players that a lot of people wondered, 'Well, what's he doing there?' This was a good, honest, hard-working hockey player – no dirty stuff, just a guy who came to play the game every day, every shift – and again, he had such good Christian values.

It was a clash of two cultures, us against them. This was about much more than hockey. This was the whole perception that we grew up with about the Iron Curtain. It was the Berlin Wall, it was against East vs. West, it was about spies and all that. The Canadians were a bunch of beer drinking hockey players and everybody was pretty confident that the Russians were going to get their come-uppance, and lo and behold...I remember very well Phil Esposito in Vancouver on national television saying how disappointed he was with the booing that the team was getting. That to me was a significant turnaround, not only for Canadians but for the team itself. He said, look this is a good hockey team and we're trying our best and what we need is for Canada to get behind us and support us. He said it so well. I can still see the sweat pouring off his face and he's trying not to use his locker room language because he knows he's on national TV, but he got the point across very well.

It was the goal that was seen around the world and that one feat should earn Henderson a place in the Hockey Hall of Fame. That one feat by itself. It's such a memorable event, such a significant event in Canadian history – and I'm saying in *Canadian history* – not just Canadian *sports* history. There are other people who have gone on to the Hockey Hall of Fame that are remembered, not for an accumulation of X number of years, but because of something great that they accomplished. This was a great accomplishment and I understand that Paul Henderson actually jumped on the ice – I don't think anyone gave him a little pat on the back to get out there – he was eager to get out there. I think he deserves that sort of recognition. It was that important to Canadians.

There were a lot of Paul Hendersons in the National Hockey League when you look at it. But you also have to look at this – Paul was around when there weren't over two dozen teams in the NHL. He was a respected hockey player before 1972.

Sidney Crosby's Olympic goal was important but I can't remember where I was when Sidney scored that goal. I suspect I was in my rec room. I watched the game, I remember the game, but it doesn't pull at my heart strings as much as Paul Henderson's goal did. It was a different time. The circumstances were so completely different, the cold war doesn't exist to the degree that it did back then. It's not the same Russia that we knew in the seventies. A lot of Canadians now pick a team to cheer for and maybe our favourite player on that team is a Russian. '72 was the first real clash of the titans in the sporting arena. It's already been done. It will never be duplicated. The stars were in alignment, the planets were lined up one behind the other.

❧

A Knockout

Bruce Patacarik ~ Ottawa, Ontario

Picture this...seven mechanics, three machinists, two carpenters and one auto body man from four shops at Ottawa Hydro gathered together to watch a hockey game!

Three of the guys were diehard Canadien fans and the rest a mixture of Toronto and Chicago fans.

On the day of the BIG game, one of the carpenters smuggled in a portable TV which we hid upstairs in the repair shop mezzanine where we stored extra parts and materials and it also doubled as a small lunchroom.

When the game started, we all took turns sneaking upstairs to watch the game. Being the newbie, I got the lookout position, watching for the boss and warning them if anyone of authority approached. When anyone came by, we all remained very quiet until they went past.

If asked where everybody was, I was to tell them they were out on a vehicle road test...worked every time!

Of course with the cheering and comments being shouted out at the various plays, the boss found out what we were up to by the 3rd period. He was not a hockey fan but said the Canadian team better beat those "Red Buggers."

When the big goal came, one of the machinists was so excited that when he jumped up to cheer he forgot he was sitting right under a 12" steel I beam, jumped and knocked himself on the head. We all began laughing until we realized he was out COLD!

We then began to revive him and when he came to, he was still disoriented so the boss sent two fellow workers with him to the hospital to get checked out.

They returned to work three hours later announcing he had suffered a mild concussion. The boss gathered us together and told us not to ever utter a single word to anyone...EVER!

Post Script: The machinist did not remember a thing that had happened and asked, 'Who won the game?'

57

We Won Coach...Seriously!

Dave Pendlebury ~ Fenlon Falls, Ontario

The day of the winning goal scored by Henderson, I was a high school football coach. At the end of the second period, even though all activity had ceased so the students and teachers could watch the game, I had to leave and head to the football field. Canada was losing 5-3 at the end of two periods. I thought, well, it's been a great series anyway.

I got to the field and a lot of students knew that I was an avid fan of the series and they were walking behind the bench after the game concluded. They were saying, 'Hey sir, Canada won 6-5 and Henderson scored the winning goal.' I kept saying, 'Yeah, right.' I thought they were putting me on. After about the sixth or seventh kid had told me, I said, 'Is this serious?'

The team we were playing was a secondary school from Lindsay, Ontario. Their bench was down the way and we were beating them fairly handily. When word about Henderson's goal got to their bench, their team was leaping up in the air and cheering. It looked kind of odd for a team that was down in the football game to be so happy!

❧

58

It's A Canadian Thing

Jim Prime ~ New Minas, Nova Scotia

Prime is the author of several sports books including How Hockey Explains Canada which was co-authored with Paul Henderson.

I was driving an American colleague to the Halifax International Airport where he was catching a return flight home to Minnesota. I resented having to drive him because I was unable to watch Game Eight. But I was able to listen to it on the radio and the more I listened the more nervous I became.

As I approached the airport, Paul Henderson scored the winning goal. Not only did I have trouble controlling the car, but also I immediately got a nosebleed. There I was one hand on the steering wheel and one pushing Kleenex into my nose. My American colleague gave me a puzzled, slightly bemused look. 'It's a Canadian thing,' I said proudly.

❧

Henderson's Exclusive Stick Club: The Gamer

Scott Raithby ~ Dartmouth, Nova Scotia

It's hard to believe that I've had a small piece of Canadian history for almost forty years. While it's provided great joy to my family and me, it's almost been as enjoyable to share the stories that accompany the stick as well as share the stories about my parent's journey to Moscow for the '72 Summit Series.

My dad played a year with the Hamilton Tiger-Cats but he was a veterinarian, mostly for large animals. He came home from work one day and told my mom that he had bought tickets to go to Moscow to watch hockey. I actually have the receipt for the tickets that they bought. I think my mom thought he was off his rocker. There were a lot of logistical issues because they had to have passports done up and visas to be obtained and so on. I do remember them having to get politicians involved to fast track things, but they made it.

Mom and dad went as part of a tour group. A whole planeload went from Toronto. We grew up in Goderich, Ontario. Dad started out his practice in Lucknow, Paul Henderson's hometown, and moved to Goderich in 1965. They flew out of Toronto and over they went. At first, I thought they flew with the team but Paul set me straight on that. The team was already there when the fans showed up.

It's my understanding that some of the players' wives stayed at the same hotel as my parents. I was in grade five or six at the time – 11 or 12 years old – and when the games were on, classes shut down and all the kids went to the auditorium and watched them on TV. My dad was actually on TV during a Foster Hewitt interview. It was totally surreal when I think about it now. Here's my dad halfway around the world in 1972 and I could see him. He was in the background while Foster was conducting an interview. When they returned after the series, the neighbourhood people had got together and made a big 4' x 8' sign on our front lawn that said 'WELCOME HOME TV STAR.'

The school shut down and we watched every game on TV, and thinking about it now it just brings chills to me. I was at the right age, 11 or 12, and hockey was big in our family. I remember that we'd go down to the Maple Leafs games with dad. We were very good friends with Frank and Shirley Orr. Frank was the longtime writer for the Toronto Star. We called them Uncle Frank and Aunt Shirley. My mom went to nursing school with Shirley, so that connection became strong. Whenever we went to Toronto, dad would get tickets from 'Uncle Frank' and we would go to the games.

They really enjoyed Moscow. It was a big culture switch, from North America to the Soviet Union, and you have to remember this was in the middle of the Cold War too. Mom and dad never indicated to us kids that they didn't feel safe, but there was a real language problem. In the middle of Red Square my dad jumped up and yelled into the crowd, 'Anybody speak English?' and they actually got a university student there to guide them around Moscow and show them the sights. He ended up wanting to come to Canada to study, but I don't think he was ever allowed to leave Russia. So that's how they got to know a lot about Moscow.

There were also a lot of organized tours. They went to the Bolshoi and the opera because mom was big into the arts. Dad probably went and slept but mom enjoyed it. They never ever talked about having been watched. I know some of the others did feel that way. They definitely felt that they were guided – 'You're going here, you're not going over there. You're walking this way, not that way.' But there were never any guns or threats like that.

We never spoke to them at all while they were over there. There was such a time difference. I was the oldest at 11 or 12 and my brother was 10 or 11 and my sister would have been about seven. I remember they had to get the babysitter on very short notice. I also remember that in the subdivision where we lived, the VLA (Veteran's Land Act), everyone was very supportive. 'Whatever you do, go!' they said. They weren't gone a whole long time. The four games were played over seven or eight days

– so not even two weeks, maybe 12 days or so.

I remember them saying that at the games they were very boisterous, shouting and cheering and clapping, and the Russian fans didn't know what to think of that. All of a sudden there were these few Canadians – compared to the home fans – and these few Canadians were making all the noise. They whistled occasionally which was the European thing to do. Mom would say that there was the odd vodka and other drinks in the stands too, so that might have been a little taboo, but they were certainly noisy and I think the players responded to it.

Dad said later that Phil Esposito stood out and Brad Park too. You don't hear a lot about Brad Park. We actually have Park's stick from the game as well as Paul's. They got it the same way. They asked for it and they handed it to them.

After Henderson scored the winning goal, the players on the ice were celebrating and whatnot and from what I understand, dad reached over or leaned over the glass – got Paul's attention, and basically said, 'Paul can I have your stick?' and Paul handed it up to him. Even my mom makes reference to Paul handing him the stick. I believe Brad Park's stick was gotten as he was leaving the ice. I do remember dad saying that he left the stadium with both sticks underneath his coat. He had a big long black coat.

He later autographed it in Moscow to my brother and me at a reception at a hotel later on that night. I have a great picture of them. Dad's standing there with a cigarette in his hand and his arm around Paul. Coming home from Moscow, my parents took the stick on the airplane. It didn't go in the cargo hold!

Just before he passed away, my dad met with Paul, who was speaking at a church engagement in Lucknow. This was 15 years ago now and dad took the stick and Paul actually signed it again. I couldn't ever find the signature and actually it was (CBC reporter) Colleen Jones who pointed it out to me. It's very faint and hard to see.

I met with Paul in Halifax and Truro, NS during the Jersey Tour * and when I talked to him and showed him the stick he said, 'Yup, that's a stick from Moscow. That's one of them.' It's my understanding that there are five sticks and he knew where four were. I guess he didn't know where the fifth stick was until that time, I'm not sure. I'm just going by what my mom and dad say – that this was the stick he scored the goal with. If you look at the stick that he's got in his hand when he scored and you look at our stick, the tapes all match. Can I say that this is *the* stick? I'm just going by what mom and dad told me so...But Paul did say in the trailer 'That is definitely one of my sticks from Moscow.'

It's a privilege and honour to have it. I've tried to contact the Hockey Hall of Fame to tell them I have it. I'd really like for it to be there. I realize they already have one and I believe they think they have the one that's real too. But they've never contacted me to verify it or discount it. Would I give it up? I don't think so. It would always be in my family. But I'd loan it to them. I really enjoy it when people ask to see it. Sure I have it and I own it or whatever, but I'm just thrilled that people want to hold it and look at it. When they ask, I say, 'Sure.' The only thing that I ask is that they don't put it on the ground or try to flex it, which is a natural instinct.

Were they parents of the year for bringing this stick home to us? Here's the story. They brought it home and I remember sitting at the dining room table. They brought out the two sticks and I think my brother and I thought, 'Yeah right, you guys just grabbed a couple of sticks and signed them' because Paul's penmanship is very good. It's not like today's stars where it's just a bunch of hen scratchings. And even for him to write on there – 'Best wishes from Moscow, Scott and Wade.' It's so clear and legible. So I think both Wade and I thought, 'Yeah, right...This is mom's handwriting.' And I've often thought about it too over the years. Is it really real? Is this really his? Of course I had no reason to doubt my parents but this is a national historic artifact. I remember mom and dad had it in their games room hung on the wall. They had a beautiful house in Grand Bend so whenever mom would show it off on garden tours and things like that, the sticks came off the wall and were hidden.

Since I obtained it in the last few years after my parents were gone, I still ask myself, 'Is it really Paul Henderson's?' so when he went on this Jersey Tour, I was just itching to talk with him. I was thrilled when I found out they were coming to the East Coast.

How did we decide who got Paul's stick and who got Brad Park's? When my mom passed away a couple of years ago, my wife and I had gone up to Ontario. We were cleaning up the family house, going through stuff and I just said to my brother, 'What about the hockey sticks?' and he said, 'Well, what do you want?' And I said, 'I want Paul Henderson' and he said, 'Ok, I'll take Brad Park.' They almost got left behind. We sold the house so we were distributing everything to my brother and my sister and then taking our stuff. We had hired a shipping company and on the last sweep through the house we almost overlooked them, my wife had wrapped the sticks up. Close call. She wasn't shipping them, they were going in the car with her.

I've been in touch with the company that authenticated Paul's #19 jersey, to give me a value on this because they're the only people around that I know that will appraise it. As for the insurance – how do you get coverage for stuff like this!? I told my insurance company that I was worried after a picture of Paul, me and the stick appeared on the front page of the Chronicle-Herald and when I called her that Monday, she said 'I thought you'd be calling me.'

Editor's note: In 2011, Paul Henderson's Game winning jersey from 1972 was purchased for $1.2 million and later taken across the country for viewing with Paul making personal appearances.

❦

In Living Colour

Paul Robichaud ~ Shippagan, New Brunswick

The Honourable Paul Robichaud, Deputy Premier, Minister of Economic Development, Minister responsible for la Francophonie and Government House Leader in New Brunswick.

I was born and raised in a very big family and we were not very rich. I remember we had a black and white TV at that time. My uncle, who was doing pretty well, had just bought a color TV, so all my family and even a number of neighbors were there to watch the game. It was a packed house and we all celebrated when Henderson scored that famous goal. That was the first time that I ever saw a color TV. It was a wonderful, wonderful day for Canada! And wonderful for hockey too.

🍁

Gliding On Euphoria

Peter Scarth ~ Georgetown, Ontario

Once upon a time in Moncton, New Brunswick, on September 21, 1972, Bruce Campbell Scarth was born. At that same time, there was a little hockey tournament happening between the USSR and Canada. This tournament better known as the Summit Series, was not going well for Canada and dad, a.k.a. me, needed to travel to Newfoundland to install a new Photo System at Tooton's in St. John's. The flight to St. John's from Halifax, was not a happy time onboard Air Canada. It was in the last few minutes of the sixth game and it was tied, meaning the USSR would win the tournament. This is the information we had as we listened "on the ground" before takeoff.

At this dramatic point, the captain announced that he had to turn off the radio while taking off, so he said he would tell us the outcome after at cruising altitude, It was the LONGEST WAIT EVER, almost as long as the wait for Bruce to arrive – and he was several weeks late! Anyway, the intercom finally clicked on and everyone waited for the inevitable news. At first the captain said, very solemnly, that the game was over. Everyone was waiting for the bad news and then he SCREAMED into the microphone that Henderson had scored in the last few minutes and Canada had WON. The whole plane load of passengers and crew jumped up in the air and we glided on euphoria into St. John's. The rest of the story happened when ALL of Canada watched Paul Henderson do it all over again in Game Eight! WOW!!!!

Two Worlds Collide

Fred Sgambati Jr. ~ Wolfville, Nova Scotia

Fred Sgambati Sr. was a Canadian Sportscaster for 28 years. He worked for CBC Radio, CBC TV, CKFH Toronto, publicity director for the CFL and was the radio voice the Vanier Cup. The Fred Sgambati Award is presented annually to a member of the news media who has made a major contribution to the growth and development of Canadian Interuniversity Sports.

As a boy growing up in Scarborough, Ontario as the son of sportswriter Fred Sgambati Sr., I may have a different perspective on the '72 Summit Series. For my Dad, it was a huge moment in his career. He was a humble man and loved what he did. He was curious about the Russian team. When he first saw them practice he was very impressed by their skating ability and saw that they had a different style of play. As the series played out, emotion became an intangible that proved to be the difference. And Team Canada had the emotion!

I recall that before Game Eight, my dad had been reporting on an officiating controversy. The Russians wanted two West Germans to officiate, which didn't sit well with Alan Eagleson and Harry Sinden. There was talk of boycotting the final game. That issue was resolved that afternoon, but it certainly added to the tension of the series.

For me, the final game was the day two worlds came together. It was really the first and maybe only memory that school time became *Canada* time. There was so much anticipation, and I recall how they rolled in a 200 pound black and white TV on a trolley. We're in *school* watching *hockey*!

I'll never forget the cheering and eruption when Henderson scored!

After the game, my dad called from Russia. My mom couldn't believe how excited he was. He talked about how it all came together and that it was an overwhelming experience. The game was returning to Canada!

*

Taking A Fall

Jim Sheldon ~ Guelph, Ontario

I remember exactly where I was during the last game of the Canada-Russia series in 1972. I was attending University of Guelph as an undergrad at the time. One of my professors – definitely not a hockey fan – insisted on the completion of a science lab the afternoon of the game. We had a radio and were quietly listening as the game progressed, all the while frantically trying to complete our assignment. I finished up in the latter part of the third period with Canada down by two goals. My residence was all the way across the campus so I began to run. I had made it half way across the commons, when a roar went up from every residence indicating to me that Canada had scored. We were down by one.

As I arrived at my residence, a second cheer went up...tie game. By the time I got to the common room and the TV, every student on my floor had beaten me to the choice viewing locations. In a fit of desperation, I convinced a girl from my floor to link arms and stand on the back of a chair occupied by another student. From this vantage point we watched the dump-in by Cournoyer, followed by Henderson getting checked in the corner. After getting up and making his way to the net, Henderson found himself all alone in front of Tretiak with the puck, and jammed it in. Well, those sitting down jumped up, including our chair owner, and the girl and I fell backwards into a sea of people. I remember this as if it were yesterday. To this day, including watching the Blue Jays win their first World Series, this was the greatest sports memory of my life.

On an aside, Henderson played shortstop for a baseball team in

Goderich, Ontario. I played for St Mary's, Ontario and we would run into his team in tournaments. He was a good athlete but I remember meeting him for the first time and thinking, 'I thought he'd be taller...'

❧

Henderson's 'Hat Trick'

Carol Ann Simon ~ Toronto, Ontario

I remember the '72 Summit Series well. I was in the eighth grade attending the Homeland Sr. Public School in Mississauga, Ontario. Being a figure skater, we didn't always get along with hockey players due to scheduling ice time and ice conditions, but I was excited about the '72 Summit Series.

They played all the Russian games over the PA system except the eighth and final game which they showed on TV in our home room.

It was 5-3 heading into the third period and people were freaking out. Paul Henderson scored the game winning goals in Games Six and Game Seven, so we were hoping that we could will him to do it again for the final game.

I remember classmates saying, 'I'll eat my hat if Henderson scores.' Another commented that he would eat his ruler.

Well, he did it again, and we all celebrated and my classmate mockingly chewed on his ruler.

It was the most excitement in my young life. I'm not sure much more was done at school that day!

❧

Parking Lot Pride

Allan Simpson ~ Kelowna, British Columbia

Simpson is the founder and editor of the publication Baseball America. He was inducted into the Canadian Baseball Hall of Fame in 2011.

I distinctly recall listening to Game Eight on my car radio while parked for a couple of hours in a shopping mall in Everett, Washington, where I was attending school at the time. The game was unavailable on local TV, and I remember being the only person in the parking lot who exalted in Canada's historic and stunning triumph – perhaps because most shoppers were oblivious to the fact that a hockey game of major international significance was going on at the time.

At any rate, I consider the NHL's improbable 6-5, come-from-behind win over the Russians that day the pinnacle moment in Canadian hockey history. It was much like most Americans pointing to their country's signature hockey moment as the historic U.S. win over the same Soviet team in the 1980 Olympics. That win ultimately led to a gold medal. I listened to that game, too, on radio, while living at the time, oddly enough, in Vernon, B.C.

There are plenty of other ironies involved in the two historic North American hockey wins. Both events began with low expectations – in Canada, because of the country's feeling of invincibility when it came to international hockey, particularly with a team stacked with NHL all-stars; in the U.S., because its team of amateurs was a decided underdog against Russia's hockey machine. Just as Canada believed it would steamroll the

Russians in 1972, Americans believed its team would be steamrolled eight years later.

While Canada didn't dominate in its eight-game Summit Series as most Canadians expected it would, it did manage to finally subdue the Russians four games to three (with one tie), thanks to game-winning goals by Paul Henderson in the final three games of the competition on Russian soil. It was a real eye-opener for most who followed hockey, particularly Canadians, when Russia routed Canada in the first game of the series played in Montreal. The Russians went on to take what appeared to be an insurmountable 3-1-1 series lead. At that juncture, it was equally unexpected when Canada managed to turn potential embarrassment into the country's ultimate sporting triumph by pulling out both the final game and the series in dramatic fashion. Dramatic even for a lonely soul sitting in a parking lot.

❖

Teammate, Friend, Babysitter

Darryl Sittler ~ Kitchener, Ontario

Darryl Sittler played in the NHL from 1970 to 1985. He played 12 years for the Toronto Maple Leafs and became team captain in 1975. He was the first Leaf to reach the 100 point mark that year. In the inaugural Canada Cup, he scored in overtime to win the final series for Team Canada over Czechoslovakia. He continues to hold the NHL record of 10 points in a game. In 1989 he was elected to the Hockey Hall of Fame.

Back in 1972, Paul Henderson and I were teammates on the Leafs. At that time, I was 21 and it was my second year with the Leafs. We became friends and generally drove to practice together.

Well, when Paul and his wife Eleanor flew to Moscow for the '72 Summit Series, my wife Wendy and I agreed to look after his three young daughters. School had started, so it was easier for the girls if we stayed at their place and I was in preseason training.

Really, the whole nation was caught up in this series. In the beginning, we expected a clean sweep. The games were more exciting as the series went on. I believe Phil Esposito's speech in Vancouver played a big role in the eventual outcome.

By the time Game Eight had arrived, I was in Vancouver as we were in the middle of our exhibition season. That afternoon, we watched the game at the Hotel Vancouver with the rest of the Leaf team. I was thrilled for Paul, he became a Canadian hero with that goal.

When Paul and Eleanor returned home from Moscow, they were

greeted with congratulatory signs all over their front lawn.

Paul and I remain friends to this day. In fact, last year we were invited to go to Israel for a week for a hockey event and we had a great time together.

❦

A Missed Opportunity

Alan Tambosso ~ Calgary, Alberta

My most vivid memory of the '72 Series is not of "the goal" but of one of the earlier games in the series. I was 14 years old at the time and living in a small town just north of Toronto.

Our family of five was in the car heading to the cottage for the weekend on the evening of the game in Winnipeg. My older brother and I kept urging my father to drive faster and faster.

Finally, my father asked, 'What's the hurry?' We told him that we wanted to get to the cottage soon so that we could watch the game. When my father asked, 'What game?' we told him that the Russians were playing Canada in Winnipeg.

'Oh, that game. I was at the dentist earlier this week and Dr. Galvin asked if I wanted two tickets to the game in Maple Leaf Gardens. I told him no, because I didn't think you guys would be interested.'

Once we got to the cottage, the five of us spent the evening huddled around a 12 inch black and white television with a rabbit ear antenna and a very blurry picture, watching the game, knowing that but for our father's misunderstanding, we might have been able to see the series live in Toronto earlier in the week.

❦

A Steel At $1,000 Per Minute

Dave Thoebold ~ Hamilton, Ontario

I was working at Stelco in the No. 1 Bloom Mill in Hamilton, Ontario during the series. Due to our mill's style of steel production, there were always guys on break, so we asked management if we could rig an antenna on the roof for a TV in the lunch room. They agreed as long as we policed ourselves to prevent workers not returning to their job when it was their time. This arrangement worked out well throughout the series. Production and communication in the mill was via a telewriter at the soaking pits that was viewed in several locations throughout the mill.

At approximately the 15:00 minute mark of the third period of Game Eight, the telewriter announced that the rolling of steel was stopped and told everyone to go watch the game. At the time we thought that it was just luck, that something had happened to halt production so near the end of the game, but as we later learned, management in our mill was also caught up in the excitement of this series and had ordered production to halt till the end of the game. This is significant in that in 1972, downtime in that mill cost Stelco $1,000 per minute.

When one of the most important and biggest companies in Canada allows production to halt, even for five minutes, to watch a hockey game, it shows how much a part of Canada's culture this series had become. I'm sure there are other similar stories across Canada from other industries waiting to be told.

A Communal Happening

Melanie Wade ~ Toronto, Ontario

Growing up in hockey-obsessed Toronto in the '60s and early '70s did little to prepare me for the most momentous occasion in my short life, also known as the 1972 Summit Series. The opportunity for our best players to take on the best that the USSR had to offer was what all Canadians had been waiting for, for far too long. Our national pride was wrapped up in our hockey superiority, as it was our game, after all.

My introduction to professional hockey came on my eighth birthday at Maple Leaf Gardens in March, 1967. The Toronto Maple Leafs defeated the New York Rangers 3-2 on their way to their fourth championship season of the decade. This was a tradition in Toronto, of course. (Please do not remind me that this seemingly routine feat would not be repeated through this much later date, perhaps not again in our lifetimes.)

The all-knowing Toronto media forecast a sweep – eight wins for Canada – with the Soviets lucky to score a few goals here and there. Game One in Montreal saw our boys jump out to an early 2-0 lead, and viewers across Canada felt vindicated for the years of humiliating losses to the team in red. It was now apparent that those losses were because we were not represented by our best players. Despite the quick offensive burst by Team Canada, however, something was amiss. Team USSR was more than a little bit quicker, executed passes more brilliantly, stymied our heroes with superb goaltending, and by the end of the game, our national pride was severely bruised by a 7-3 loss. How could so many "experts" have been so wrong?

Fast forward to Game Two in Toronto where Team Canada

rebounded with a solid 4-1 victory. Game Three in Winnipeg ended in a 3-3 tie. Team Canada's 5-3 loss in Game Four to a better USSR team turned out to be the pivotal game in the series. Continuous booing from the Vancouver spectators led captain Phil Esposito to respond with both a rousing tribute to Team USSR and a heart-felt protest against the lack of support for Team Canada who, after all, were doing their best against the talented, cohesive visiting team. This set the stage for the upcoming four games in Moscow with the upstart Soviets ahead 2-1-1.

Few hockey enthusiasts could have predicted the crazy twists and turns the series would take behind the Iron Curtain. Because of the time difference, these games occurred during the school day, so the thousand strong student body of Milneford Junior High School gathered in the school's auditorium for the viewing of Game Five. Despite the taciturn Soviet crowd, who were drowned out by a much smaller and enthusiastic Canadian contingent, our boys lost 5-4 after building an early three-goal lead. To many in the Toronto media, the series was all but over.

But somehow, our boys rebounded in Game Six with a thrilling 3-2 victory. Similarly in Game Seven, Team Canada responded with a brilliant 5-4 effort with Paul Henderson scoring the game winner in the closing minutes. Bedlam broke out in the school auditorium. It was the most exciting moment of my life. The series was now tied at 3-3-1 with a decisive Game Eight on the horizon.

I was looking forward to another communal happening in the auditorium for Game Eight when it was announced that students were welcome to return home to view the upcoming historic event. As we lived only a few blocks from campus – and owned a colour TV, unlike the small black and white variety at the school – I opted to view the game from the comfort and close proximity of my family room. Today, I harbour mixed feelings about this decision since, yes, I did get a much better view, but, no, the experience lacked the ambiance and sheer excitement of being part of the crowd.

Nevertheless, Game Eight proved to be one of the most anxiety ridden and thrilling experiences of my early adolescence. My mother was home, and together we endured the ups and downs of this momentous occasion. With my stomach in knots, I do not remember too much about the game until the late third period. With Team USSR ahead 5-3 after two periods, I had begun to resign myself to a Canadian loss in the series, painfully trying to accept that we would lose to a better team.

But then, early in the third, Team Canada roared back with two goals to tie the game. In the closing minutes, I humbly acknowledged that the Soviets were a much better team than any of our experts had ever given them credit for and that Team Canada had shown tremendous fortitude, tenacity, and determination to even the series on enemy soil. A tied series was not a bad result.

Not long after these consoling thoughts ran through my mind like a movie, the puck was in the net, and our hero, Paul Henderson was being swarmed by the entire team. It would have been difficult to write a more dramatic script. I remember jumping up and down and screaming and hugging my mother repeatedly. Of course we *were better* after all. We were Canadian. This was a comforting conclusion...for the time being.

Media Rookie Scores Big

Alex J. Walling ~ Halifax, Nova Scotia

Walling is a major sports analyst in Atlantic Canada. He contributes weekly to a sports column on TSN. Walling was Atlantic Canada's first TSN sports reporter. He reports daily on Halifax Information Radio (97.9 FM radio).

I was twenty four at the time and working at CHNS Radio in Halifax. I'm in Edmonton covering a softball tournament with the local Dairy Queen team when the first Summit Series game is played in Montreal. It's the end of August which is when it started. They played four games, then took a little break and went to Russia. I went to my boss Ian Morrison, and said, 'Come on Ian, let me get to see one of the games.' So after awhile he called me and said, 'Yeah we're going to let you see a game.' I said, 'Great! I'm going to Toronto!' The game was that night in Toronto. So I said 'great, I'm going to see them play in Toronto!' He said, 'No, we couldn't make arrangements in Toronto.' I said, 'Oh, ok, nothing wrong with Winnipeg!' Cause I'm thinking Canada. He said, 'No, not Winnipeg either. So I said, 'Great Ian, I'm going to Vancouver, the only city I haven't seen!! Thank you!' He said, 'You're not going to Vancouver.' I said, 'Christ, where am I going, Morrison?' He said, 'You're going to Russia.' That's how I was told.

The biggest shock to everybody was that hardly any of us in the media saw the winning goal. The reason for that is that first of all there was no press box for us. They made a press box up for Foster Hewitt and they made a press box for Howie Meeker. The Russians had no press boxes. This was '72 so all of us media types were put in one area. Picture us sitting in front of the glass in a section from the blueline in to Ken Dryden. We had a great view of Dryden. So we were way on the other end of the ice, and down at the bottom of the stands. We were in the first, second and third rows so you couldn't see too much. Our faces were practically against the glass.

Ok, this is what happened when the winning goal was scored. First of all, the red light did *not* go on. From where we were, we didn't know if he'd scored or what had happened. And 3,000 Canadians couldn't make any noise because they didn't see the red light come on. They were all on our side of the building. That's number one. Number two, with all the legs and people on the ice we didn't see anything. And yet we knew something big happened because the players came over the boards to congratulate the guys, and especially Henderson.

I only saw the winning goal on my new TV in December, at the end of the year. It always makes a big impact when people say, 'Well, there you were in the great Canadian moment when Henderson scored the big goal!' And I have to tell them, 'Guys I never saw the goal.' *(Editor's note: Goes into his best Hewitt voice)* '...and Henderson has scored for Canada – and Walling doesn't see it!'

My best memory of that game is of numbers 16 and 13: (Vladimir) Petrov and (Boris) Mikhailov. The score is 5-3 for the Soviets. They are on a two-on-one break and they're coming over the blueline. They do that amazing passing back and forth, back and forth...and what I remember is that they got Kenny Dryden out of position with all those passing plays...I think Bill White was the defender...and they shoot. They have an open net – half the net open and – the score's going to be 6-3 and the game is going to be over. Well, they shoot over the net! And then I believe Cournoyer picks it up, the Road Runner, and the next thing you know it's 5-4. So to me that one play was crucial. Instead of being 6-3, it's 5-4. That is the thing I remember most about it.

You're going to like this one because I like it! With 34 seconds left, Canada scores. I look around and I see 17,000 people at this Luzhniki Arena and I say to myself: *Ok, decision time Walling. They are obviously going to take Tretiak out of the net. So I'm going to have a chance to see either a tying goal or maybe a great ending right in front of me. But I want to go down and I want to talk to the team after.* And I'm thinking all this in a matter of five seconds. Do I go now? Do I stay? I go.

I head off and go up the stairs. I've got my trusty Sony 102 tape recorder and I head down – and by the time I get behind Dryden's net there's five seconds left – that's with the off-sides, with the whistles, and so on. So there I am. Then all of a sudden the game is over. Well there are only two of us waiting to talk to the people! Paul Henderson comes out and he's immediately taken by CTV – not CBC, but CTV did games – and Bill Goode Jr., I think, interviewed him. Now for whatever reason, today this wouldn't happen, but they only talked to him for around forty-five seconds or a minute. Maybe microwave time was very, very expensive from Russia in 1972, that's the only thing I can think of. Anyway, so he's finished with them and he comes walking toward the two of us. Two young guys – and Paul Henderson himself! The other guy with me was Brian Williams, then working for CHUM Toronto and now working for CBC. Now Williams knew him a little bit because he had followed the Maple Leafs. Williams and I put our microphones in front of him. Brian asked the first four or five questions 'Hi Hennie, your feelings?' or something like that. Anyway, the bottom line was we talked to him for six minutes. Six minutes! Now where's the rest of the Canadian media contingent? They're stranded in the 17,000 people! One of the best moves I've ever made in my career!

There's a series on video tape and at the end of Game Eight, as the two reporters come out, you can see my shadow clear as a bell talking to Henderson and my daughter says, 'Dad, you had bushy hair then.' People say 'How did you do that?' And the answer is that the other guys were caught in the 17,000.

Some people say that Paul seemed to be in a trance. Maybe he was in a trance with other reporters, but Williams and I noticed nothing special. I mean he was happy. Delighted. I don't think he could believe that he scored three winning goals in a row. Totally amazing. Almost four! I found him wonderful. His demeanor was great – and after our six minutes, I had all the questions I needed and I headed off and the other thirty or more media guys descended. I have no way of proving this, but I believe I might have been the youngest media guy there. Most of the guys were veterans from Toronto – Bill Stevenson, Fred Sgambati Sr., Jim Hunt and so on. So many from Toronto, I was so lucky to get in there.

People ask me, 'Alex J., what did you do for two weeks in Russia?' I tell them I stayed in my room and waited. I filed twice a day, once before and once after the game. I'd go to practice in the morning and we'd talk to players. I had a phone in my room and as soon as I got back there I had to feed CP. Get this, it would take anywhere from an hour to four hours to get an outside line, so I had to stay in the room. I had no choice. I had to feed Canada both before the game – 11:00 in the morning, whatever time it is here and after the game – 10:00 at night... every day – and people can't believe it, but I had no choice.

I was tied up talking to players and heading back to my room. But I know there were a lot of parties among the Canadians.

After it was all over, the Russians were down about it, but years later I met Tretiak at a golf tournament in Digby (NS) and he summed it up pretty well. He said, '1972 good series for hockey.' Now he wasn't supposed to be able to speak English and he had his interpreter right there but I asked him, 'Look, you were classified as a Junior B goaltender and the day that the scouts saw you – John McLellan and Bob Davidson – they classified you as a *terrible* Junior B goaltender. What gave them that impression?' And he smiled and said, 'Oh, one of the players had bachelor party. Tretiak have a hangover at practice.' It was so funny. Because I can imagine these two Canadians just judging, not knowing – *My god that guy's terrible.* Then he said, 'Look, there was '72 and '75. '72 great for all hockey. '75 against Canadians, great for Tretiak.'

I had a great chance. Now mind you, I am the first one to tell you: never did I expect that this would become the greatest hockey story in Canadian history. None of us knew that. I interviewed Russians. I went up in the crowd with an interpreter and talked to about ten Russians in Game Five in Moscow. Overwhelmingly – I mean like nine out of ten people – when I asked, 'Who's the best Canadian?' they said, 'Esposito.' And he was. Now mind you it was before Game Six so Henderson hadn't scored that winning goal and I certainly didn't get any reaction after the last one but it was Esposito by far at that point.

Then I talked to Foster Hewitt and I said, 'Sir, you've been through a lot since the 1920s and so forth, why is it you have a problem with (pronouncing) Cournoyer?' (Foster, in his nasal tone) 'I know, Alex. I know. I know. I don't know why. I can name Mikhailov and Bodunov and Lebedev and I get them all right but that one has got a mind set for me, and I keep saying Con-oy-ER instead of what his name is, Conouryer.' Foster was a real gentleman. *'And Conorir, Coooroyer, Cournooyer, scores for Canada.'* But it was all good.

The last day, we're there in the morning for workouts and somehow

Brian Williams had a special pass that I think guys covering NHL teams got. With my CP and CHNS credentials, I would probably have gotten it but didn't ask for it. Anyway, we're walking through the arena entrance at 10:30 in the morning and a Russian guard says, 'Stop!' he points to William's pass – that I didn't have – and he motions Williams to go, me to stop.

Brian says, 'Brian Williams, CHUM sports, this guy comes with me!' As if the guard knew what Brian was saying. The guy just looks at him. Brian says again, louder: 'Brian Williams, CHUM Sports, this guy comes with me!' The guy moved over and let me through.

Good memories. Hard to believe it was forty years ago. Once at a press conference Alan Eagleson announced, 'You can't question me on the Summit Series unless you were there.' He said that because he didn't want or expect any questions. I stood to ask a question and he barked, 'Were you there?' 'I certainly was,' I said.

🍁

Espo Excels

Jim Westlake ~ Toronto, Ontario

W. James Westlake is the Group Head of International Banking and Insurance for RBC Bank.

I was in high school and had a part time job at a local trucking company, Valleyview Transport. A number of us were working in the garage. There was a small black and white TV in the office and we kept running in to see what the score was. It was looking pretty dismal but each time Canada scored in the third period someone would run out and shout. We were all fortunate to be huddled together around the TV when Henderson scored.

All these years later I still remember thinking that Phil Esposito may have played the best period of hockey ever that day, scoring the first goal in the third to start the rally and assisting on the final two. I was thrilled to join many members of that team at their 25th anniversary golf day at Devils Pulpit. I had each of them sign a poster for the event. I had it laminated and it hangs on my recreation room wall today.

❧

Skating On Thin Ice

George Willet ~ Montreal, Quebec

I'll never forget the '72 Summit Series! Canadians certainly know the impact of the hockey series, but most don't know about the history of Penta, an enterprising hockey skate company formed in 1972.

Former NHL'er Terry Harper led Penta, which produced plastic moulded hockey skates. We started the company in January of '72, raising money from investors and creating a skate prototype.

It was now the morning of the pre-game skate for Game One of the series in Montreal. You could cut the tension at the Forum with a knife. For us it was a big deal because Team Canada '72 player Mickey Redmond was going to test our prototype during the skate. He would be the first pro to test the skates.

The trial went well and I'll never forget the electricity at that game. The game didn't play out as we thought as Canada scored two quick goals, but got blown out in the third period by the Russians and lost 7-3.

The aftermath of that day was that representatives from the skate company Lange (our former employer) were in attendance at the morning skate. Four days later, we were issued a stop work injunction by Lange, claiming that we had taken trade secrets.

We vehemently denied their charge and went to court in November, where the judge ruled in their favour. We were extremely disappointed with the ruling and decided to go through the appeal process which would take place a year later.

The story moves to '73 where the judge overturns the ruling and we're back in business. We had to raise money again and we continued operations for three years. You may remember the hockey equipment company Jofa, which was a division of Swedish car maker Volvo. Gretzky and Lemieux, among others, wore their helmets. Well, they acquired Penta as part of their hockey skate line.

I guess you can say that things ended well for both Penta and Team Canada after quite a bit of adversity. Quite a series!

♦

Overtime

The Pre-Arranged Marriage

Steve Dowling ~ Hingham, Massachusetts

Steve Dowling was an America-born referee who officiated Game Two of the Summit Series in Toronto.

I got a call in early summer of 1972 from NHL Referee-in-Chief Scottie Morrison. He said that there was going to be a hockey series and that the series was going to be restricted to players from Canada and Russia. He also said that through negotiations, it was decided that no official would come from either one of those two countries. They settled on American refs in Canada and European refs in Russia.

I'm pretty sure it was the first time the NHL had played outside their league for any reason. And the Russians were on top of the world. They had won Olympics after Olympics after Olympics. And I believe there was some enterprise in that the whole concept came from one individual who kind of orchestrated the series. It was his approach to bring the powers of hockey together to play against each other – for enterprise, I'm pretty sure. That man was Alan Eagleson. His goal was to establish the NHL dominance and to dim the bright light that was on the Russians from winning the Olympics year after year, and being declared the best in the world. So the way to do that, I guess, was to have them face-off.

So to me it was like a pre-arranged marriage. That marriage was supposed to be: the Russians come over, the Russians have fun, the Russians lose, the Canadians continue on to say they defeated 'the best in the world.' Arranged marriages are between two people who have never met each other before and a third party brings them together.

Normally, an arranged marriage includes some sort of entrepreneurial arrangement that benefits a third party. The Summit Series was arranged and the two parties were supposed to be compatible to make a good series and a good game and it didn't go well right off the bat.

Training Camp

It was absolutely a lark for the Canadians. I had a couple of clippings and I forget who the lead writer at the Toronto paper was but he wrote a whole article about how this was just going to be an extension of training camp. It was just going to be an exercise. Canadians should win all eight games and if they lose one it's just because they're taking it easy. And that was very much a reflection of what was happening at the Canadian training camp. That article came out the day before the game in Montreal. The inter-squad games were fun games. You know, you go the arena Sunday night, get a bunch of guys you know and you go up and down the ice and have a beer afterwards. All of that occurred every day! They were at their training camp/fun time.

We were aware of the Russians being at the Canadian camp. The players weren't there but they had their advance party there and you'd see them frequently with a guy named Kukolwitz. He was their interpreter – a pretty well known guy. He was an interesting character, worked for Air Canada and was assigned to Russia. He spoke Russian – and I'm pretty sure he was a Canadian CIA-type spy over there. In any case if you knew he was around, then the Russians were around also, just kind of watching. They were there to evaluate the potential and come back to their players and give them the scoop and the scouting report – and maybe buoy them up a little. Probably say, 'We can beat 'em one way and that's to out-condition them.'

I had done a fair amount of college officiating in the US, and the college and high schools used two officials so I and the other three officials had done considerable officiating within that system. The other American officials, particularly Gagnon and Lee, had Olympic experience. At that time, the IIHF was a two-man system also, so for us – for all the officials, I think, both in Russia and in Canada – the two-man system was more natural than any three man system. I personally prefer one ref and two linesmen. The NHL had deemed two officials inadequate considering with the speed of the game at the pro level. With only two officials, they have to be linesmen, they're refs, they're handling the off-sides and the icings and you spend a lot of time being a linesman, watching where the puck is as opposed to watching the play. You're making sure that you're at the line watching for offside calls going both ways, so it doesn't reflect the reality of what a big game is. One ref and two linesmen is clearly superior.

The Series Begins

I was at Game One so you could see what was going on there. I did play hockey for a number of years so I had a sense in watching the game – as a hockey player, not just as an official – of the level of puck-handling, speed, and control in the first game displayed by the Russians, versus the lack of that by the Canadians. I think most people would agree.

I think Sinden deployed what were supposed to be his speedier players and his better puck handlers in the first game. And they still got outmanoeuvered. So when you see the change in the lineup where you get Parise coming in, Cashman coming in to the lineup, Goldsworthy coming in, Mikita being activated and so on, you think *well, this is a different set of players here.* There was something compared to the first one just because of the nature of the blue collar type workers that Cashman and Goldsworthy and those guys were. So you were fairly sure that it was going to be an intense game. Also, the fact was that Canada had not yet exhaled from the first game. It was my perception that when that game was over, five minutes later no one had moved from where they had been standing or sitting in the Forum. Because it was such a shock. And then you read the headline the next day – not the sports headline, but the front page headline – was *We Lost!* And that was the same headline all across Canada. So when that happens in a series like this, it's not the local team and they move on to another series someplace else. This is two countries that were embroiled in the bitterness of what was the Cold War and the nature of politics. It was the Communists vs the Capitalists and authoritarianism vs democracy and all those other things. You quickly realize *the mood's different here*!

Early in the Montreal game when Canada scored twice, the party was on. It was clear that it was a sure thing. Everyone's opinions were validated. The thinking was: *I just hope they don't embarrass the poor Russians by doing that* – and then it was like a well-orchestrated movie. Then the dark cloud approached and then the storm hit and the storm didn't subside until the end and there was even some thunder and lightning after the game when the Russians stood out there – their jaws are open, their hands are up to shake and Canadians are long gone. So it was like a movie that had a second part and you weren't too sure what the second part of the movie was going to be but clearly a dark cloud and a thunder storm were involved in that movie.

Considering all that, part of preparation for a ref is to make yourself aware of the potential, for what *could* happen. Through the whole spectrum. The whole spectrum includes the possibility that, okay, this will be another dance like the first one and the skillful, fast Russians will continue to manoeuver around the somewhat less conditioned and slightly more flat-footed Canadians. Or, what we didn't see in the first game was the typical physicality that you'd have in an NHL playoff game, and if that comes back into play and it goes over the line, then you have to be prepared to officiate a little tighter. So part of the prep is emotional, part is physical but it all revolves around the discipline to be aware of what's going on, and then invoke what you have for options.

Clearly Game Two game started off, number one, with a new lineup, number two the play was more the NHL style early on. I think there was a growing frustration from the Russians because now they're getting banged around. They hadn't been banged around for decades – maybe never. When they played in the Olympics, it was a very gentlemanly game, with a kind of prep school civility, a lot of ceremony, and a lot of honour. Typically in an NHL game, there's an element that's physical. It was totally lacking in my mind in the first game. The second game starts out physical. There's banging. No one's running the Russians like you saw in the (2012 NHL playoff) series between Pittsburgh and Philadelphia, where there were some horrific types of moves. There was none of that. No one's head got snapped back by a crosscheck to the throat but they're hitting them, you know? There's a little bit of stick work there, little irritants that were overlooked back in those day in hockey. Stick work, pushes to the back of the leg, those types of things. As long as they don't go too far, they are just irritants. They're mosquitoes and the Russians started to get irritated by that.

Then the Russians were starting to get hit hard and the frustration was building up, boiling up both on the coaching staff and amongst the players. By the end of Game Two, they had to regroup the same way that the Canadians had to regroup after Game One. We had two totally different teams in this 'arranged marriage.' The first two go-arounds in the honeymoon aren't going so well and then when you get to Game Three, not much happened. Again they were feeling each other out to see which way they were going to go for the rest of the series. I think the Russians made the adjustments by the time they got to Game Four to deal with the physicality and try to capitalize on their edge in conditioning – because the gap was narrowing. I think Team Canada had worked their way from east coast to west coast by getting in better condition each step of the way.

Officiate The Game Not The Cause

Maybe it's not stated that way in the manual of refereeing, but clearly if you are an official in any sport, your agenda has to be very neutral in terms of what the organizations that you're officiating stand for. So the Canadians are very patriotic. Every Canadian has a flag tattooed someplace on them and coming into the series and the individual games, it was a cause. Canadian pride is such a big part of their game. It's not just sticks and pucks to them. But, their cause is not *my* cause. Even if it was my cause, I'd have to avoid it and have empathy that the guys on the other side of the rink have a cause of a different nature.

For that reason you can't start to think about causes or even have an emotion that influences you in any way: *Oh, I'm from North America too*...if you start doing that, then you become a fan, you become a spectator and you're not doing what you're supposed to do. I just believe in that. If you're a graduate of Boston College you would never get an assignment to officiate a Boston College game because you're got some kind of vested interest – or an attachment to a cause – and that cause is the university that you are a graduate of. Sure the Cold War was raging, but there's enough to worry about the game and the players without having another influential agenda in the back of your mind.

The Kharlamov Incident And My Contract

Anything that you really needed to convey to the Russian players you could do through their interpreter. The one situation that occurred in Game Two was through frustration. One of Kharlamov's teammates (Tsygankov) got a penalty for a slash and that was kind of the high point of frustration. It was a legitimate call because it was a stick penalty, fairly obvious. The Russians thought *something's wrong here*. Particularly Kharlamov – or more likely the Russian coach sent Kharlamov, I'm not

100% sure how they work it – to argue. His argument was *we're getting banged around yet* we're *getting a penalty and the penalty is for stick work?* So Kharlamov comes over to me saying this stuff and I'm trying to ignore him, but he comes close enough that he bumps me.

There's not too much time left in the period (Editor's Note: the penalty was at the 19:54 mark of the second period) and it's a ten minute misconduct – and I think he just scratched his head and said, 'Well what happened there?' We had no need, no reason, to exchange or explain. It was the slashing signal – that's an international one that doesn't require words and the bump is a physical action, didn't require words either. It didn't make any difference what he was saying cause I couldn't understand, so if he was saying, 'Screw you you're an asshole and your mother's this or that,' I don't care. He bumped me and there was no real need for a lot of explanation.

When this incident occurred with Kharlamov – the bumping and the misconduct –it was right along the glass. Scotty Morrison was there and it occurred right in front of him. I could see that he was standing and saying something, and I could hear something like, 'Throw him out of the game. That's a game misconduct! Throw him out! Throw him out!' So now I've got this hesitation because I'm scheduled at the end of this series to sign an NHL contract that's sitting on his desk – so I've got this hesitation but I say, 'You know what, no, I can't go with it. I have to stick my neck out here and stick with the ten minute misconduct' – so that was it, a ten minute misconduct.

Later, I get a message in my hotel room that Mr. Morrison wants to see me tomorrow morning at 10:00 o'clock at his office in Rexdale. So I'm thinking, oh, oh, this isn't good. So I go into his office and basically sit down in front of his big desk – dead centre in the middle of it on the other side – and he said, 'I'm tearing your contract up.' And I said, 'Oh well, that was a career! Minus two days! That was good.' But then he said he was making a couple of changes in it. 'There are a couple of extra bucks in it for you,' he said. 'I want to tell you Steve that I was a fan of the Canadians last night at the game. I was watching it and my allegiance showed. My blood runs very, very red in my veins and I was out of line in advocating a game misconduct. You did the right thing.'

❦

What Harry Sinden's Barber Said...

Aron Valevich ~ Moscow, Russia

Thus far you've read 72 stories from Canadians about where they were during the 1972 Summit Series. But there's always another side to the story, and this one's from a man who lived behind the Iron Curtain and was a Russian citizen. He now lives in the United States and ironically is the barber for Harry Sinden, the coach of Team Canada in '72. His views on the Summit Series then and now come from a unique perspective.

I was 17 years old in 1972, a young man, and I was at game two in Moscow (Game Six of the Summit Series). You have to understand where I was coming from. I had my own perspective, and it was black and white. All we knew about Canadians was what we had been told. My understanding of what I remember right now is different from what I understood at that time because now I live here (Boston). I know Harry (Sinden), and I know a lot of people involved and have heard a lot of arguments. I now know what the perspective should be because now I can see both sides of it.

Capitalism Vs. Socialism

To us, Canada and America were one in the same. It was capitalism. We didn't have much in life except sports and work, and hockey was, and still is, a big deal.

When they came back from Canada leading two games to one

with one tie, we *knew* we were better than them because that's what we were told. Forget about Canadians, forget about anything. When they came here, I cannot even describe it to you. I actually later saw that documentary where Phil Esposito was talking about 'war.' To us it wasn't a war. To us it was 'Who is *the man*?' because to a lot of Russians, World War II was still fresh in their minds. Plus we wouldn't draw the word 'war' into it. To us war was a lot of dead people. My own dad was an invalid from World War 11. He was a hero of World War 11.

To me it wasn't war. It was capitalism against socialism. *Now* I understand that all the Russian hockey players were professional players. In Vancouver, Esposito responded to people who were saying that you are pros playing amateurs, what's wrong? I don't think those fans knew the lifestyle of Russian hockey players. They may have had little salary, but if they knew about that lifestyle, they'd know they were so mistaken.

Maybe they were not professional to the extent of the Canadians, because they didn't make that much money, but they were doing nothing but playing. They didn't have money but they had lifestyle and all the benefits of professional players. They were heroes, like same thing Canadian players were to Canada. It was pretty much the same except for the amount of money. But the amount of life quality, I can grant to you it was pretty much the same. But at that time we didn't think of that. To us it was those guys, which was capitalism, against socialism. Beating those guys was very important to us because it was like sport was equal to the social mentality.

My Game Six Experience

I'd been to games before. My personal favourite team at the time was Spartak Moscow and I'd been to their games and it was a small arena – much smaller than Luzhniki. Luzhniki was a huge stadium, like Wimbledon in England. I'd never been in such a huge arena in my life. Right now, thinking back, the funny part is – and again I was 17 – we all tried to behave like good boys. No one told me when I walked into the arena –'Hey there are going to be a lot of cameras. Don't yell, don't scream.' Russians don't do that, especially at that time. No, to us it was like – I cannot even describe it – it was like watching theatre. It was not like watching sport, it was like watching theatre. And as for me, I never left. I never went to bathroom, I don't even remember if we had a concession or if we could go there and buy something. I don't remember that because I never did. I never left. I never pee, I never poop. I never did anything because I was afraid to move out. I was afraid to miss anything. To me, it was just mesmerizing and it was a hell of an experience.

The Canadian fans made a lot of noise! That was another thing. That was the first time that I saw that. Some Russians were chanting 'CCCP' but that's only because someone asked them to do that – KGB. Security was crazy. No question about it. We're talking about police, we're talking about KGB – because later on I worked in the 1980 Olympic Games in a hotel where a lot of fans were staying, and at that time I learned what Russian security means.

I'm pretty sure at that time in Luzhniki Arena, stadium security was literally crazy. I think every fifth person was KGB or militia because I saw so many people in ties and plain suits. Normal human beings didn't do that! We didn't do that. A lot of people around me were like that – maybe that's one of the reasons no one talked – they were afraid to say something. If I know anything after 22 years in the United States, North American people want to know the idea of what was Russia and what wasn't Russia at that time. Was it a prison? For us it was more than prison. It was and it wasn't. I don't want to make it even more confused. It was different, a whole different story, a whole different book…

That particular game was unbelievable. I saw so may people yelling and screaming (for Canada). There weren't that many people and they made that much noise?! They brought the signs. And we just looked at them and thought – What are you, crazy? I thought they were absolutely nuts. We couldn't understand. In Russia, if you watch the old sport games you will see we react if somebody scores the goal or almost scores the goal. You see people sometimes get up and say something but it is up and down but it's never a group on the steps saying, 'Woo, woo, woo. Go Canada!' or singing a hymn to Canada or something. In the middle of Moscow and singing like that!? No one tries to shush them. They all sing together and no one said 'Sit down.' It was one of the shocks! It was huge difference. Now when I watch Bruins games, it's second nature, but when I saw that first time I cannot even describe it.

Series Turning Point

When the Canadians won that game two (Game Six of the series) in Moscow, they broke our hearts. They broke my heart, anyway. I remember talking to a guy, a buddy of mine from the Spartak Moscow games. Russians, we don't usually talk like this but I was watching with my buddies from Spartak Moscow. He was on my left and he said one thing – to me the reason we lost that game. I think the score was already 3-1 and they score and they kind of slap each other with their sticks on the legs but there was no happiness about it, they didn't act on it – and the guy said, 'You know what? They are too cocky.' I can't describe his exact phrase but if they're not so excited about it, they assume they will win. And no freakin' way! Because we saw these Canadian guys – no helmets, they look like the boxers, all their noses broke, toothless and everything and we just knew they were fighters. We didn't know or care about anything else. We just knew they were boxers the way they behaved, the way they attacked and everything. We knew they were going to fight to the end, because to them it was the same thing that it was to us. And the way our guys behaved it was, 'Oh, whatever, another goal.' My friend said, 'I just don't like that, they're not excited about it. They're not congratulating themselves enough.' What do we know? We lost that game and when he said that I didn't even say anything. He was talking loud and I said to myself, 'You know, he's right!" and when they lost it that's all I was thinking about because they were so damn sure.

After game two in Moscow it was kind of like an inflated mattress had been pricked with a needle. I wasn't surprised that we lost after that. So that's it. I saw one of the four games and Harry Sinden to me is one of my idols. If you ask me to be honest with you, I'll be honest with you. When they lost the game, it was just: *I want to go home. I want to go home, take a shower and go to bed.*

I watched Game Eight in my apartment. We didn't have sport bars like you did. In Russia we didn't have many TVs. Thanks to my father, my TV was the biggest screen, although by today's standards it was nothing. I would say I had about 12 people watching in my apartment because not a lot of people were having TVs.

To me, it was first of all embarrassing, and we talked about reasons why we lost: they were so big and strong and the average speed of puck was higher than average speed of Russian hockey player. But at that point you're looking for excuses, for explanations and quite honestly if I remember anything, it was mostly they lost because they were really, really so excited. It's like following up with sex – when you're done. You go there, win two games and practically won three games. If I had had such success on that level – and I was a barber on that level – I'm not sure I wouldn't feel the same thing. They went there and they inhale and then when they were on the plane home they exhaled. I think they never inhaled again. They never grasped the idea. What you guys did was the opposite of that.

Esposito Stood Out

I remember Esposito first of all because he was a big guy, second of all because he had the longest hair at that time. Perhaps it was kind of Beatlemania to us. I liked that because it was my style too. He was big, he scored practically in all games the first goal, and the funny part was, right now when I'm watching and I remember – he wasn't that mean like other players during the game. After the game, he was trying to take the conversations in his own hands like he's a big shot, but as a player he was incredible. I do remember the moment when he grabbed his throat and he showed like he cut his throat like he wanted to kill you. At that time I didn't speak English so I didn't understand but I do remember that.

Many, many years later I actually met him. I saw him at the bar of a sports place here in Boston. At first I didn't talk to him because that was embarrassing to me because I was kind of star struck. I saw him drinking and it was stupid of me but I yelled, 'Hey Esposito!' He looked at me across the bar and said, 'What?' And I did the same thing – I smiled and made a cutting throat motion. And he laughed! That was his reaction! It was like he still remembered that and maybe, because of my accent he could quickly remember that. Then he smiled and raised his glass and he continued to drink. The point is, I didn't know if he'd remember that incident, but years later in Boston he did.

I bet if you asked him right now he would remember. It was really interesting to me to see his reaction to that. It was just perfect.

🍁

Passing the Torch,
Henderson Cheers Crosby's Goal

Paul Henderson ~ Streetsville, Ontario

This is the story of where Paul Henderson was during the Sidney Crosby 'Golden Goal' that occurred during the Vancouver 2012 Winter Olympics Gold Medal Game between Canada and the United States.

Eleanor and I were speaking at a marriage conference in Victoria, BC. We missed the first period of the game and then we had a break and I got to watch the next two periods. The game is winding down and I'm looking at my watch and I think I'm going to see Canada win and then go back to speak.

Well, (Zach) Parise scored with just a bunch of seconds left...oh no! So Eleanor and I had to go back to speak. I said to the couples, if any of you have a radio or anything...because we had talked about the game and what we were going to do...I said if the US scores, don't say a word, but if Canada scores, please just yell it out.

So about 15 minutes into the talk, this lady stood up. 'Canada scored! Crosby scored!' The whole place went nuts! I started, just spontaneously, to sing *Oh Canada*. Everyone stood up and we all sang *Oh Canada*. Unbeknownst to me at that point, we had six American couples in there! They were so gracious, they understood our enthusiasm.

That's the only time I've led the singing of *Oh Canada*!

About The Authors

Sean Mitton

Sean Mitton has interviewed many hockey legends including Paul Henderson, Wayne Gretzky, Sidney Crosby, Yvon Cournoyer, Darryl Sittler, Mike Bossy, Eric Staal, Marc Staal and Jordan Staal.

He is the Founder of the Canadian Expat Network (CEN), the leading website for Canadians living abroad. CEN provides e-newsletters, news of upcoming events and stories of interest for Canadians living abroad.

CEN has also published a Curling e-Resource Book in partnership with USA Curling, promote Terry Fox Runs internationally and has worked with Labatt Blue on a program called "Hockey Night in the U.S." CEN is proud to have RBC Bank as a sponsor in the U.S.

Sean grew up in Georgetown, Ontario.

Jim Prime

Jim Prime is the author of fifteen sports-related books and has contributed articles to various magazines and newspapers. He has co-authored books with Canadian hockey icon Paul Henderson, baseball immortal Ted Williams and baseball philosopher Bill "Spaceman" Lee.

Jim is a rabid fan of the Boston Red Sox in baseball and the Montreal Canadiens in hockey, and points to Ted Williams, Jean Beliveau, and Paul Henderson as his sports heroes.

Jim grew up in Freeport, Nova Scotia and lives in the beautiful Annapolis Valley with wife Glenna. They have two children and two grandchildren.

Stories can be posted at www.72project.com